Let's Create

Peace of Mind

Together

Ray Penn

LEGACY WEALTH PLANNING for Minnesota and North Dakota Families

By Estate Planning Attorney
Raymond J. German

With
Robert Armstrong and Sanford M. Fisch

ISBN 978-0-9841215-6-4

© 2016 American Academy of Estate Planning Attorneys

www.aaepa.com

Contents

Preface

Robert Armstrong and Sanford M. Fisch
—Founders, American Academy of Estate Planning Attorneys

What do you want from your estate plan? If you're like many people, you want a plan that allows you to make sure the financial security you've worked hard to acquire is preserved so you can pass it on to your loved ones when you want, where you want, and in the way you want. You likely also want to make sure you minimize any taxes, court costs, and attorney's fees in the process.

However, your estate plan can go far beyond accomplishing these basic goals. Your plan has the potential to protect the financial futures of your spouse, children, and grandchildren long after you're gone. You can also use it to capture something more than your financial wealth. The right estate plan can provide your loved ones with a spiritual and emotional legacy, one that ensures your family's values, stories, work ethic, morals, and history—in short, your family's unique and powerful identity—are preserved right along with your financial wealth.

To accomplish these goals you'll need to venture beyond the confines of traditional estate planning with its narrow focus on financial assets. You'll need to identify and preserve what we like to call your family's true wealth.

How can you do this? At the American Academy of Estate Planning Attorneys we have developed a holistic approach to estate planning which we call Legacy Wealth Planning. The goal of this book is to help you understand not only the shortcomings of the traditional approach to planning your estate, but also the enhancements Legacy Wealth Planning can bring to the process. Legacy Wealth Planning can provide your family with a true and lasting legacy, one that affects hearts and souls along with pocketbooks.

In this book, you'll be taken, step-by-step, through the options available with the traditional estate planning model. You'll see how these tools, effective as they are at addressing basic concerns, fall short when the focus shifts from passing on financial wealth to passing on true wealth. You'll also see how Legacy Wealth Planning effectively addresses the many challenges faced by today's American families.

Through this book, we aim to expand your understanding of the ways in which you can provide a true and lasting legacy for your loved ones. We also trust that you'll come away from reading this book having learned some practical approaches for bringing to life your goals for the future of your family.

The American Academy of Estate Planning Attorneys is a member organization serving the needs of attorneys committed to providing their clients with the best in estate planning. Through the Academy's comprehensive training and educational programs, it fosters excellence in estate planning among its members and helps them deliver the highest possible service to their clients.

Robert Armstrong is the founder of one of the most successful estate planning practices in the country and a co-founder of the American Academy of Estate Planning Attorneys. His expertise in estate planning has made him a sought-after authority, and he has been quoted in the Wall Street Journal, Newsweek, U.S. News & World Report, and Money Magazine. He provided estate planning expertise for the bestseller, Terry Savage on Money. He is also the co-author, along with Michael E. Gerber and Sanford M. Fisch, of The E-Myth Attorney: Why Most Legal Practices Don't Work and What to Do About It. Robert and Sanford also collaborated on a book to teach attorneys how to effectively help their clients in the new digital age, Dominate Your Market, The Attorney's Complete Guide to Online Marketing and Social Media and co-authored over 14 books on Basic Estate Planning with attorneys around the country.

Sanford M. Fisch is the CEO of the American Academy of Estate Planning Attorneys. In addition to building a prominent estate planning law firm and co-founding the Academy, Sanford has developed innovative approaches to helping families prepare for a comfortable, crisis-free inheritance. He is responsible for collaborating on the strategic direction of the Academy, and, through his work with the Academy, he has become a recognized leader and sought-after advisor and consultant to law firms throughout the U.S. Sanford is the co-author, along with Michael E. Gerber and Robert Armstrong, of The E-Myth Attorney: Why Most Legal Practices Don't Work and What to Do About It.

A final note: This book reflects the opinion of the American Academy of Estate Planning Attorneys. It is based on our understanding of national trends and procedures, and it is intended as an overview of the benefits of the Legacy Wealth Planning process. Although we believe that you will find this book to be a helpful resource, we recommend you do not base your own estate planning on the contents of this book alone. You'll want to review your estate planning goals with a qualified estate planning attorney.

Introduction

We would like to start our journey together by telling you, congratulations! You are probably asking yourself, *"For what, what have I done?"*

The very fact that you are reading this book means that you are taking a step that a majority of our fellow Americans consistently fail to do. You are choosing to tackle two pretty frightening issues—death and taxes—and put an estate plan in place, or improve your existing plan.

Contrary to popular belief, death and taxes are not the only important issues you face when planning your estate. It seems strange then that they have been the sole focus for a majority of estate planning professionals and the estate plans that are ultimately created. The focus of this book is to highlight and examine some of the important challenges that may arise in the event of your disability or death. These life events, particularly disability, have not traditionally been addressed in the context of estate planning.

Traditional estate planning can be effective for ensuring that your financial wealth is distributed to whom you want, when you want, and in the manner you want. It has provided tools for ensuring that this distribution is handled by the person you want. It has even provided ways to avoid or minimize Death Probate, Living Probate, and estate taxes. However, estate planning attorneys have started a new conversation, one that goes beyond traditional estate planning.

Our world is ever-changing, and the needs of our clients are constantly evolving. Today, our clients are encountering new legal issues that can have a dramatic effect on them, their spouses, their children, and their heirs. For instance:

In the event your spouse chooses to remarry, how can you protect your estate and ensure that your life savings makes its way into the hands of your children and grandchildren?

Given the high rate of divorce, how can you protect your children's or grandchildren's inheritances in the event their marriages fail?

In today's litigious society, how can you minimize the dissipation of your legacy by legal claims against those you leave behind, or even by your loved ones' own poor judgment or financial missteps?

How can you leverage your retirement savings to provide in the best possible manner for your spouse, children, or grandchildren?

In addition to these and other financial issues, there is an increasing and urgent need to address how our clients' non-financial wealth is treated in the estate planning process.

This has prompted the development of a new way to meet our clients' needs, called Legacy Wealth Planning. Legacy Wealth Planning is designed to go beyond the traditional focus on financial assets to capture and pass on your true wealth, in a way that provides lasting security to your loved ones. Through the Legacy Wealth Planning process, the focus is not only on your net worth, but also on your values, wisdom, life lessons, family history, and precious memories, including your treasured personal items and family heirlooms.

Our mission is to introduce you to a more holistic view of family wealth, one that reaches beyond finances, and to help you discover how this shift in focus can change everything you've ever thought and heard about estate planning.

About Raymond J. German

 As an attorney in Minnesota and North Dakota, Raymond J. German provides a wide range of estate planning services to his clients, with a primary focus on helping them provide for the security of their loved ones, reduce estate taxes and avoid or at least minimize the costs and delays of probate, all with a well-crafted estate plan. Mr. German defines the mission statement for the German Law Group as *"Helping one family at a time pass on values, beliefs and finances, that can be shared for generations to come."* Mr. German is well aware of the growing importance of estate planning and dedicates himself to informing the public of the need for careful attention to their specific situations. He is a frequent speaker on a variety of estate planning topics, regularly presenting educational seminars for the public as well as private groups.

Mr. German was awarded his Juris Doctor Degree from the University of North Dakota School of Law in 1973. He is a member of the American Academy of Estate Planning Attorneys.

His other areas of practice include: Basic and Advanced Estate and Business Planning, Trust Administration, Probate, Incapacity issues, Special Needs, and Value Based Planning.

About the German Law Group

At the German Law Group, we provide practical and creative solutions to the myriad of challenges faced by our clients. We are estate planning attorneys practicing in North Dakota and Minnesota. It is our mission to provide our clients with unparalleled life and estate planning services.

At the German Law Group, we have a philosophy about working with our clients. Because estate planning is an extraordinarily complex area of the law, we make it our business to maintain the highest level of expertise required, to handle not only the areas of law and the scenarios that are discussed in this book, but also the many other challenges our clients encounter while planning their estates.

We believe that the success of our law firm rests on these core elements:

- Passion for helping families plan
- Strong comprehensive knowledge of estate planning issues
- Experienced staff
- An ongoing relationship with your family
- No surprises

Our mission and our passion in Legacy Wealth Planning is to make a difference, one family at a time.

Chapter 1
Traditional Estate Planning Only Goes So Far

Planning is bringing the future into the present so that you can do something about it now.

—Alan Lakein

When you think about what you want an estate plan to do for you, what things come to mind? Of course, you want to be able to pass on your wealth to your loved ones or to the charitable institutions of your choosing, but this is just the tip of the iceberg. When it comes to planning for what will happen after your death—and even what will happen during your lifetime, if you become disabled—there is so much more to take care of than simply doling out your possessions. What else should an estate plan do for you?

When we talk to our clients, they voice five main concerns that they'd like to address through the estate planning process:

1. Passing on their hard-earned wealth to their heirs without court involvement, and without a large percentage being taken out in the form of attorney's fees

2. Avoiding unnecessary taxes, not only during their lifetimes, but also during their heirs' lifetimes

3. Avoiding the loss of their nest egg to the high cost of a nursing home or assisted living facility

4. Protecting not only their estate, but also their loved ones, from creditors and predators after they're gone

5. Passing on wisdom, values, and life lessons to their children, grandchildren, and the generations that follow

Traditional Estate Planning Focuses Exclusively on Financial Assets

Unfortunately, not all of these concerns are addressed by the traditional estate planning process. The vast majority of attorneys, accountants, and financial planners have been taught to focus on protecting their clients' material possessions from probate and taxes. That's it. Under the traditional estate planning model, the focus is on what happens at the time of your death, and the only issues addressed are:

- Who gets what you own?

- When and how do they get it?

- How can these transfers be achieved at the lowest possible cost?

What are the tools that are used under the traditional estate planning model to address these issues?

- The Last Will and Testament

- The *"Bare Bones"* Revocable Living Trust

- Joint Ownership of Property

- Transfer of Property Using Contract Rights

- No plan at all

Each of these tools has its legitimate purpose (except for not planning at all, of course), and you will notice that we have devoted a chapter to fully explaining the specific benefits and drawbacks of each traditional estate planning method.

Traditional Estate Planning Neglects Important Real Life Issues

The truth is that these estate planning tools are only sufficient if you are limiting yourself to a traditional estate plan. Doing this ignores some of the most important issues faced by real-world families. Things like what happens if you become disabled during your lifetime, or what will the impact be when your spouse, children, or grandchildren inherit your property—and how can you protect them even after you're gone?

Traditional estate planning doesn't leave room to address issues that are oftentimes more divisive to a family than paying too much in taxes or having to navigate the court system.

You may know siblings who haven't spoken for years because they couldn't agree on who should get their parents' wedding album or their grandmother's tea set. Even worse, traditional estate plans often dump assets on children and grandchildren, only to see them wiped out by divorce, eaten up by lawsuits and creditor claims, or spent carelessly by the heir themselves. Then there's the guilt that many families feel over the fact that they didn't take the time to capture the memories, wisdom, and life stories of their parents before they were lost forever.

Let's take a look at the tools traditionally used by Americans to plan their estates, starting with the Last Will and Testament.

Chapter 2
A Will Might Not Be the Way

Where there's a will, there's a way.

—Proverb

The Last Will and Testament, which most people just call a Will, is the first thing that many people think of when they hear the term *"estate planning."* While a Will is an important part of a complete estate plan, it is by no means the only estate planning method available. Nor is it usually the best-suited tool to address all the estate planning needs of today's families.

What Does a Will Do?

A Will is an effective way to take care of the following estate planning tasks:

- Naming a Personal Representative, also called an Executor, to make sure that the wishes contained in your Will are honored

- Distributing your property to the people or institutions of your choice after you pass away

- Controlling the manner in which your Beneficiaries inherit your property

- Giving direction as to how any debts and taxes are to be paid

- Nominating a guardian to care for your children in the event that both you and the children's other parent pass away before the children reach adulthood

- Providing for the management of your children's property in case they are still minors when you pass away

A Will is effective as a basic estate planning method because it lets you control who gets your property when you pass away and in what form that property passes to your Beneficiaries.

A Will Comes With Drawbacks

A Will has a number of drawbacks that can make it a substandard instrument for today's families unless it is also accompanied by some additional estate planning tools. What are some of the potential drawbacks of using a Will as your only estate planning tool?

- **A Will Only Takes Effect After You Pass Away.** Because of this, there is no way to use your Will to plan for disability during your lifetime.

- **A Will Has to Go Through Probate.** Probate is the court-administered process through which your Will is proven to be valid and through which your property is transferred to the Beneficiaries you named in your Will. The process can be expensive and it can take time. Often, while Probate is pending, your family does not have access to your assets.

- **A Will Is a Public Document.** Probate is a public process. In order for the process to even start, your Will has to be filed with the court. At this point, your Will becomes public record and can be accessed by anyone who is interested in its contents. Then, notice is published in the newspaper that Probate has started. This means that people who might not have even known you had a Will may suddenly become aware of it and decide to take a look at it, either out of curiosity or for more harmful reasons.

- **A Will Is Relatively Easy to Contest.** A Will has to be probated. So, in order for your property to be transferred to your Beneficiaries, a court process is required. For an unhappy family member, or an unscrupulous creditor, it's relatively easy to file the necessary paperwork and dispute a Will during the Probate process. In fact, it is much easier to jump in on a court proceeding, like Probate, which is already in progress, than it is to go through the time, expense, and trouble of initiating a lawsuit. Whether or not the Will contest is successful, it will cost your estate time and attorney's fees.

A Will Is Not Enough

Of course, even the simplest of Wills is better than no plan at all. In order to have a truly effective estate plan, you need more than just a Will. Not only does a Will fall short in each of the above categories, it also does nothing to protect the financial interests of your loved ones as they go on to live their lives. Lastly, a Will does not capture and pass on your memories, your family history, or any part of your legacy that is more than merely financial.

Chapter 3
The Basic Living Trust: High Maintenance Estate Planning

Put not your trust in money, but put your money in trust.
—Oliver Wendell Holmes

Like a Will, a Living Trust is a method for distributing your property after your death. Unlike a Will, however, a Living Trust can be effective even before your death. This means you can use it to plan for the possibility that you may become disabled at some point in the future. Unlike a Will, a Living Trust does not have to be probated, so it can help your property transition to your Beneficiaries more efficiently and more economically. While it offers more benefits than a Will, a basic Living Trust has its drawbacks.

How Does a Living Trust Work?

A Living Trust, like any other Trust, involves three basic roles:

1. The Trustor, also known as the Grantor or Settlor, is the person who creates the Trust and transfers assets into it.

2. The Trustee is the person responsible for managing the Trust assets according to the written instructions established by the Trustor.

3. The Beneficiaries are the people who benefit from the Trust.

When you establish a Living Trust, you'll likely occupy all three roles. As Trustor, you will create the Trust and transfer assets into it. As Trustee, you will manage those assets, and as Beneficiary, you will be the one who—initially, at least—benefits from the Trust. So, even though you've established a Trust and transferred property into it, you still retain complete control over the property, and it is yours to use as you see fit. A Living Trust is revocable, which means that you can change the terms of the Trust, or even cancel it altogether, any time you like.

Why Set Up a Trust?

You may wonder why you would transfer property from yourself to yourself, for your own benefit. When it is first established, your Trust is simply a *"standby device."* Imagine it as a treasure box into which you place your property. As long as you're alive and healthy, it is business as usual as far as your property is concerned. You still control it, you get all the benefits from it, and you can do with it as you please.

What is significant about putting your property into a Living Trust is that now, instead of your name on the title to the property, the property is owned by the Trust. Property that is not titled in your personal name is not affected by your disability or death. This is one key reason that a Living Trust can be a more effective estate planning tool than a Will.

What Happens If You Become Disabled?

What if you become so ill that you can no longer take care of your own finances and property? Or, what if you're in an accident and you're injured to the point that someone else needs to manage your financial life for you? With a Living Trust, you initially name yourself as Trustee, but you also designate a Successor Trustee to take over in case of your disability or death. If you're married, this will likely be your spouse.

If you can't manage your own financial affairs, your Successor Trustee will step in and manage the Trust assets, according to the instructions in your Trust agreement. This is assuming, of course, that your Trust is properly drafted and is kept up-to-date. If your Trust contains mistakes, inaccurate language, or inconsistencies, then your Successor Trustee could be forced to go to court to get permission to take control of your assets.

Assuming your Living Trust is well-written and up-to-date, it should help you avoid Living Probate, the costly and time-consuming process through which a court appoints a guardian or conservator to coordinate your care and the management of your finances.

What Happens at Your Death?
When you pass away, your Successor Trustee, with the help of an attorney, will take control of your Trust assets, pay any legitimate final bills and debts, and manage and distribute the property in your Trust according to your instructions.

Tax Planning With an AB Trust
If you are married and your estate is large enough, your Living Trust should also have provisions to avoid estate taxes. The Trust will be divided into two Sub-Trusts, often called Trusts A and B. With the proper language in the Living Trust document, you can minimize your estate taxes.

When dealing with an AB Trust, it is important not to confuse the A side with the B side. The A side is where the assets of the surviving spouse go; the B side represents the assets of the first spouse to pass away. An easy way to guarantee that you will never mix the A side up with the B side is to remember that *"A"* stands for *"Above Ground"*—it is the survivor's side. The *"B"* in B side, on the other hand, stands for *"Below Ground"*—it always belongs to the first spouse to pass away.

How Does It Work?
Imagine you and your spouse are the Trustors and Co-Trustees of a Living Trust. You have both acquired enough real estate, savings, investments, and life insurance policies to be concerned about estate tax planning. Wisely, you have asked your estate planning attorney to include tax planning provisions in your Living Trust.

Now, assume your spouse is the first to pass away. Within a few weeks after this happens, you'll pay a visit to your estate planning attorney who will divide your Trust into an A Trust and a B Trust. The A Trust belongs to you. It is revocable, and you retain complete control over the assets in the A Trust.

The B Trust becomes your deceased spouse's Trust. It is irrevocable, and it is used to hold assets up to the estate tax exemption amount for the year in which your spouse passes away. You may act as Trustee of the B Trust, and you may use and benefit from the property held by the B Trust, but you won't be the owner of that property. In return, the property in the B Trust will not be included in your taxable estate when you pass away. This is true no matter how much the Trust property increases in value during the time that elapses between your spouse's death and your death.

If it sounds complicated, that's because it is. If recent history has taught us anything, it is that estate tax laws are unpredictable, and the exemption amounts are constantly changing. If you have enough assets to be concerned about future estate taxes, a Trust that contains inadequate tax provisions, or none at all, can cause Uncle Sam to take an unnecessary bite out of your loved ones' inheritances.

The Drawbacks of a Traditional Living Trust

There are five basic reasons why most Living Trusts fail:

1. **Poorly Drafted Documents.** A poorly drafted Trust will not live up to expectations. Many Living Trusts are form documents that are drawn up quickly using an online program, or maybe even drafted by a lawyer who doesn't focus on estate planning and therefore doesn't know to include many important features.

   Failure to include effective AB Trust language is one way in which a poorly-drafted document produces an ineffective Living Trust. Another common Living Trust problem is failure to include a

Health Insurance Portability and Accountability Act (HIPAA) authorization. With the advent of HIPAA, doctors and hospitals are under a strict obligation to allow only individuals you authorize to have access to your medical records. Without the appropriate language in your Living Trust, your Successor Trustee would not have access to your medical records and might have to go to court to have you certified disabled before he or she can take over the management of your Trust assets. The result of this is time, expense, and frustration—just what you were trying to avoid by establishing a Living Trust in the first place.

2. **No Protection Against Real-World Issues.** A basic Living Trust, even if it is well-drafted and contains the appropriate tax language, may not offer long-term protection for your spouse and children after you pass away. Once Trust assets are distributed to your spouse, either outright or by becoming part of the A Trust, those assets are vulnerable to creditors' claims. They are also vulnerable in the event your spouse remarries and later divorces. Your spouse's future ex could walk away with part of the assets meant for your family, and this could be beyond your spouse's control.

What about your children? A basic Living Trust does not protect them against creditors or divorce, either. It also fails to shield them from their own poor decision-making, whether that comes in the form of overspending on life's luxuries or from the darker problems of substance abuse and addiction.

3. **Lack of Proper Funding.** Simply setting up a Living Trust is not enough. After the Trust is established, property must be transferred, or *"funded,"* into the Trust so that it can be managed by your Successor Trustee if you become disabled, and so it can avoid Probate.

The most common reason that Living Trusts fail is that they're not properly funded. Unless you have a unique, long-term relationship with your estate planning attorney, you likely don't have anyone watching out for you to make sure that the appropriate assets are transferred into your Trust at the right times. Even if the initial transfers are made, that might not be enough. You need vigilance to maintain your Trust so that it will work for you when you need it.

Consider this: Even if you initially transfer your home into your Living Trust, what happens when you refinance? It is routine for the mortgage company to require you to take the home out of the Trust, and place it back into your individual name, just for the refinance. What if you forget to transfer the house back into your Trust once the transaction is completed? Now one of your largest assets is left outside the protection of your Trust. This means it is beyond the reach of your Successor Trustee in the event you become disabled, and it is subject to Probate when you pass away.

Assets that are inadvertently left out are beyond the protection of your Trust, which means that your Trust has not performed as intended.

4. **Failure to Keep Up With Legal Changes.** What happens when tax laws change or when a new estate planning strategy becomes available that could benefit you and your family? Unless you are an estate planning lawyer or a tax specialist yourself, or you have an ongoing relationship with your estate planning attorney, you likely will be completely unaware of any new developments.

   This is true in the HIPAA example above. Many families have outdated estate planning documents that, because of legal changes, no longer work as intended. The sad thing is that most of these people will remain unaware that there's a problem until it is too late.

5. **No Way to Capture Your Non-Financial Legacy.** It is important not only to protect your financial assets and to pass them on to your loved ones in the most efficient, effective manner, but also to ensure that your non-financial legacy reaches your heirs. In fact, the latter is likely to be a much more important concern for you and your family. Your

non-financial legacy includes things like your treasured memories and family stories, your morals and values, and all those things that you truly hold dear in life and would like to pass along to your children and grandchildren. Unfortunately, a basic Living Trust is simply not capable of recognizing your non-financial legacy, let alone passing it on to future generations. With a basic Living Trust, there is a risk that the things that are most important to you could disappear right along with you, and be lost forever.

The basic Living Trust is another example of how traditional estate planning succeeds at addressing some needs, but falls very short of addressing all of the concerns you and your family likely have.

Chapter 4
Yours, Mine, and Ours: Joint Ownership

No man acquires property without acquiring with it a little arithmetic also.

—Ralph Waldo Emerson

There are four ways one can potentially own property together with one or more other people:

1. Joint Tenancy with Rights of Survivorship (usually referred to as *"Joint Tenancy"*)

2. Tenancy by the Entirety

3. Community Property

4. Tenancy in Common

Joint Tenancy With Rights of Survivorship

Joint Tenancy is the form of joint ownership that is most commonly used for estate planning purposes. When people own property as Joint Tenants with Rights of Survivorship, upon the first owner's death, all of his or her interest in the property transfers immediately to the surviving owner(s). This transfer happens without the need for Probate.

In fact, you might already own property in this manner and not even realize it. Married couples who co-own a home often hold title to that home in Joint Tenancy. Other property commonly held in this manner includes bank accounts and motor vehicles.

You don't have to be married to own property in Joint Tenancy. This form of co-ownership is often used by life partners, family, and friends in an effort to avoid Probate. However, there are a number of potential problems that come along with using Joint Tenancy as an estate planning tool.

Joint Tenancy Only Avoids Probate Once
Let's use you and your spouse as an example. If the two of you own all of your property in Joint Tenancy, and you pass away first, then ownership of the property immediately transfers to your spouse. With this transfer, you have successfully avoided Probate.

At this point, your spouse owns everything in his or her individual name. What happens when your spouse passes away? Unless he or she has taken additional estate planning steps, the property will have to go through the public Probate process before it can be transferred to your heirs.

Joint Tenancy Means that You Lose Control of Your Assets Upon Your Death
When you choose Joint Tenancy as a method for avoiding Probate, you lose the ability to protect your spouse and children after your death. Again, assume that you and your spouse own all of your property in Joint Tenancy. If you are the first to pass away, complete ownership transfers to your spouse. This leaves your spouse, and all of your property, vulnerable.

If your spouse owes money, then there is a risk that his or her creditors could access the entire value of the property for payment of the debt. Further, your spouse can transfer the home to whomever he or she pleases, which may become a particular concern if your spouse remarries. Your spouse may choose to hold all the property in Joint Tenancy with his or her new spouse.

In the event of a divorce, the new spouse could be awarded the property or an interest in it. Even if your spouse remains happily remarried until his or her death, the property will transfer to the new surviving spouse, effectively disinheriting your children.

Joint Tenancy May Mean Tax Problems for Married Owners

When you and your spouse choose Joint Tenancy, you may unknowingly lose an important estate tax advantage. As with Probate, this issue does not become apparent upon the death of the first spouse. Instead, for married couples, property in Joint Tenancy passes to the surviving spouse outside of Probate and free of estate taxes. It is only when the second spouse passes away that estate taxes become a concern, and you might owe more than you otherwise would have.

Each person who has a large enough estate at death to owe estate taxes is entitled to have a portion of their property excluded, or passed on without taxation. The amount of this exclusion can vary from year to year, and with appropriate estate planning, married couples can combine their individual exclusions. When spouses hold property in Joint Tenancy, though, they are normally not allowed to apply both of their exclusion amounts to their estate. This, however, has become less of a concern due to the *"portability election"* made available in the most recent legislation (See Page 98).

Estate taxes don't apply at the death of the first spouse because of the marital deduction, which lets one spouse pass all of his or her assets to the other spouse without paying estate taxes. The problem with Joint Tenancy is that, at the first spouse's death, property owned in this manner is transferred outright to the surviving spouse. This means that the entire value of the property is included in the estate of the survivor. So, the first spouse's marital exclusion as to the property is lost. The result is that, upon the death of the second spouse, estate taxes will be calculated on property which otherwise might escape estate taxation if other estate planning methods were used and/or the *"portability election"* being properly made.

Joint Tenancy May Mean Tax Problems for Unmarried Owners

Even if the owners of property held in Joint Tenancy are not married to each other, tax issues can arise. When you create a Joint Tenancy with someone who is not your spouse, the IRS might view this as a taxable gift. For example, if one owner provides the whole purchase price of property held in Joint Tenancy, then he or she is considered to have made a gift of half the value of the property to the non-paying owner. This is common when people add their kids to the title on their homes.

If the property in question is real estate, then the creation of the Joint Tenancy triggers the gift tax. If the property is a joint bank account or a U.S. savings bond, then the gift tax isn't triggered until the non-paying owner uses a portion of the asset.

Is gift tax due under every circumstance? No. There are certain gift tax exemptions available. Each year you are permitted to give away up to a certain amount, which is called the annual exclusion. If you give a gift that exceeds the value allowed in the year the gift is given, you are required to file a gift tax return, and you may owe gift tax on the transaction. Gifts in excess of the annual exclusion are applied against your lifetime estate and gift tax exclusions. Therefore, if your gift falls within one of these exemptions, you will not have to pay tax on the transfer.

Joint Tenancy May be a Risky Financial Move

Each of the owners of property held in Joint Tenancy owns an equal, undivided interest in the property. This makes your interest in the property vulnerable to the actions of the other Joint Tenant(s).

For example, if there are two co-owners, then you control your half of the property and your co-owner controls the other half of the property. If your co-owner declares bankruptcy, owes taxes, gets divorced, or loses a lawsuit, half the value of the joint property could be lost. What's worse, you could be required to sell the property so that the proceeds can be used to pay off your co-owner's obligations.

Tenancy by the Entirety (Not Recognized in Minnesota and North Dakota)

About half of states recognize a special type of Joint Tenancy that can only be used by married couples. It is called Tenancy by the Entirety, and if you live in a state or own property where this option is available, you can elect this ownership option. Certain states limit the Tenancy by the Entirety option to real estate owned by a couple, while in other states, the option is available for personal property as well. Currently, Minnesota and North Dakota do not allow property to be owned in this manner.

In addition to allowing you to avoid Probate on the death of the first spouse, Tenancy by the Entirety may also be useful for protecting your property from certain debts that were not incurred jointly by you and your spouse. However, it still carries with it many of the drawbacks of Joint Tenancy addressed above, including the same estate tax concerns, and the fact that Probate becomes an issue at the death of the second spouse.

Community Property (Both Minnesota and North Dakota are Non-Community Property States)

Neither Minnesota nor North Dakota recognize Community Property. The nine states that do recognize it are Arizona, California, Idaho, Louisiana, Nevada, New Mexico, Texas, Washington, and Wisconsin. In Alaska, couples can choose to have some or all of their property treated as Community Property by signing a contract to that effect. Only spouses can own assets as Community Property, and, unlike Joint Tenancy, this ownership option does not carry with it a right of survivorship. This means that, absent additional estate planning, Community Property does not avoid Probate.

Tenancy in Common

The final type of joint ownership is Tenancy in Common. Available in all states, Tenancy in Common does not carry with it the right of survivorship. Since property held in this manner does not transfer to the remaining owners outside of Probate, it is not commonly used as an estate planning tool. When two or more people own property as Tenants in Common, they each own a percentage of the property, but the percentage held by each owner does not have to be equal. Generally, it is presumed that each co-owner holds an equal share, however that presumption may be challenged if it is shown that each contributed unequal amounts.

Joint ownership of property in Minnesota and North Dakota, particularly through Joint Tenancy, may seem like a simple way to avoid Probate, but it carries with it complications and unforeseen consequences. While it might make sense as a portion of your estate plan, it is a poor stand-alone option.

Chapter 5
Splitting Heirs: Beneficiary Designations

Plans are nothing; planning is everything.
—Dwight D. Eisenhower

There are certain types of assets for which you can designate a Beneficiary outside of your estate plan. When you designate a Beneficiary, you are giving that person the right to receive all or part of the asset at your death without the need for Probate. Assets that commonly allow for a Beneficiary designation include:

- Life insurance policies

- Retirement accounts, such as 401(k)s and IRAs

- Bank accounts and other assets with a Pay on Death (POD) or Transfer on Death (TOD) designation

Types of Beneficiaries

There are three types of Beneficiaries that you can potentially name:

- Primary Beneficiaries are the first set of individuals entitled to the asset when you pass away.

- Secondary Beneficiaries become entitled to the asset if no Primary Beneficiaries outlive you.

- Tertiary Beneficiaries receive the asset if all Primary Beneficiaries and all Secondary Beneficiaries pass away before you do.

Potential Complications

Designating a Beneficiary for certain assets can be a simple way to avoid Probate, at least with regard to those specific assets, but there are certain complications that can arise. These include:

1. **The Potential to Disinherit Loved Ones.** If you designate only one Beneficiary for an asset, but want other loved ones to share in the property after you've passed away, those other loved ones are disinherited. Assets for which you have designated a Beneficiary will only be distributed to those people. It is necessary to keep up with your Beneficiary designations and update them directly with the appropriate institution when you want to add or remove a Beneficiary.

2. **The Potential for Probate.** If you designate a single Beneficiary who predeceases you, the asset in question will be included in your estate, and may have to go through Probate before it can be distributed to your remaining loved ones.

3. **Lack of Control by Your Will or Trust.** If you have designated a Beneficiary, and that person is living at the time of your death, then the asset in question is not controlled by your Will or Trust. Simply stating in your Will that you want to add an additional Beneficiary to your life insurance policy or retirement account will not be effective to do so.

   If you update your estate plan to add or remove Beneficiaries, you will not only have to change your Will or Trust, you'll also need to contact each institution where you hold an asset with a designated Beneficiary to update your selection.

4. **Potential Limits on How Assets Can Be Distributed.** When it comes to Pay on Death accounts, certain financial institutions require that, if you name more than one Beneficiary, the account must be distributed to those individuals in equal shares. This eliminates your ability to assign different shares of the asset to different Beneficiaries, and

may result in your inability to distribute the funds in your account as you desire.

5. **No Estate Tax Planning.** Assets for which you have designated a Beneficiary are still counted as yours for estate tax purposes. Simply designating a Beneficiary will not help you with estate tax planning.

Aside from these potential complications, it is only possible to designate Beneficiaries for certain types of assets outside of an estate plan. Without further estate planning, your remaining assets will be subject to Probate and possible estate taxes.

Chapter 6
Failing to Plan Is Planning to Fail

Everyone gets organized at some point, they just might not be around for it.

—Sue DeRoos

Not having an estate plan affects you and your loved ones in a number of ways. First, without a plan, you lose control over what happens to your property at death. Second, if you have minor children, you lose the ability to name a guardian to care for them in the event of your death. Finally, without a disability plan, you will need a court-appointed guardian or conservator if you become mentally incapacitated at some point during your life.

How Your Property Is Distributed

When you pass away without a Will or Trust, it is called dying *"intestate."* If you have no Will and no Living Trust, then your property likely will have to go through a court administration. This process is similar to Probate (which is what happens when you leave a Will), except that, without a Will, you do not control who will inherit your property.

Instead, your probate property will be distributed according to default state laws, called *"intestacy statutes."* Each state's intestacy statutes are different, but they all have two things in common: they are a one-size-fits all solution, and they assume that you want your property to go to your closest living relatives.

Even if your friends or family members know what you wanted, without a Will or Trust, these wishes won't be honored. There are few exceptions, if any, under intestacy statutes for wishes expressed anywhere except in a valid estate plan, just as there are no exceptions for special circumstances, or for the needs of certain loved ones or pets.

Because intestacy statutes vary from state to state, the way that your property is distributed can vary widely, depending on factors such as your state of residence at the time of your death and your family situation. For example, if you live in Minnesota or North Dakota and you are married with joint children when you pass away, your spouse will get 100% of your estate, and your children will be entitled to nothing.

What about if your spouse brought one or more children of their own into the marriage and you passed away intestate? In Minnesota, your surviving spouse would receive the first $150,000 plus one half of any balance of your intestate estate. In North Dakota, on the other hand, your spouse would receive the first $225,000 plus one half of any balance of your intestate estate.

Ancillary Probate

If you own property outside your home state at the time of your death, then lack of estate planning can cause your loved ones even more of a headache. Not only will the property in your home state have to go through court administration, this will also be necessary for property you own in other states. This means the added time and expense of dealing with the courts in each applicable state, and an even greater chance that your property won't be distributed as you would have intended. Property in each state will be distributed according to that state's intestacy laws, creating the potential for several different sets of Beneficiaries.

Guardianship of Minor Children

If you are the parent of young children, one of the most important aspects of estate planning is the ability to nominate a guardian for them. When you create a Will, you can name a person of your choosing to care for your children if both you and their other parent pass away before the children reach adulthood. If you pass away, your choice of guardian will need to be approved by a judge, but this is normally a quick and routine procedure.

When you pass away without an estate plan, there is no way for you to nominate a guardian for your children. Instead, if your children are left without parents, anyone who wants to serve as guardian can petition the court for the role. The decision as to who will care for your children is then in the hands of a judge whom you and your family don't know, and who has no way to know what your preferences would be or to get any guidance from you. It is the responsibility of the judge to make a decision that's in your children's best interests. However, the judge's choice of guardians might not be one that you would agree with or approve of.

Living Probate

One component of an effective estate plan is incapacity planning. Consider what would happen if you experienced a stroke, a debilitating illness like Alzheimer's, or an accident. In this situation, you might lose the capacity to manage your own assets, make your own medical decisions, or otherwise live your life independently.

With effective incapacity planning documents in place, you can nominate a trusted loved one or friend to take charge in case of your mental incapacity. This person would then be able to manage your finances and make medical and legal decisions on your behalf. With an incapacity plan, you can also communicate, in writing, your preferences concerning medical treatment.

If you become mentally incapacitated without such a plan, your loved ones will need to go to court to have a guardian or conservator appointed to manage your finances and make decisions concerning your medical and personal needs. This court process is called Living Probate. It is often expensive, it exposes your medical status and other private information to debate and discussion in court, and there is no guarantee that the guardian or conservator ultimately appointed by the court will be someone you trust or wish to have in control of your personal affairs.

Your final affairs will eventually be settled, whether or not you make an estate plan. Without a plan, though, your family will be subjected to added time, expense, and uncertainty in settling your affairs.

Chapter 7
Of Mice and Men: The Failings of the Traditional Estate Plan

I was planning to be a baseball player until I ran into something called a curveball. And that set me back.

—Ben Chandler

Robert Burns is quoted as saying, *"The best laid plans of mice and men often go astray."* This can be especially true in the arena of traditional estate planning. One of the main purposes of engaging in estate planning is to be able to pass on your wealth to future generations in the way that you see fit. Most people want to do this without the intervention of the court, without paying more in taxes than is absolutely necessary, without exposing their private affairs, and without having others interfere with the estate plan they've so meticulously put together.

All too often, though, traditional estate planning methods fail to anticipate the *"curveballs"* and, in so doing, invite outside intervention. This kind of meddling in the plans that you thought were so carefully laid can serve to forever alter the legacy you had intended to leave for your loved ones. Tragically, by the time your traditional estate plan starts to fall apart, you are often either incapacitated or have passed away, and it is too late for you to step in and take action.

What are some common ways that traditional estate planning invites intervention? Let's take a look:

Traditional Estate Planning Does Not Adequately Anticipate Mental Incapacity

Traditional estate planning methods often offer either no planning or inadequate planning for mental incapacity. What if you were to enter the latter stages of Alzheimer's disease, suffer a stroke, or have a debilitating accident? If you had only a partially-funded bare-bones Living Trust or your documents did not contain a Health Insurance Portability and Accountability Act (HIPAA) Authorization Form, your estate plan could be compromised. Your family might have to go to court to have a guardian or conservator appointed to manage your affairs. This process is known as Living Probate, and it can be expensive and time consuming.

Further, the appointment of a guardian or conservator means that you lose control over who makes decisions concerning very important and personal aspects of your life. Often, your spouse is appointed to make these decisions on your behalf. However, if your spouse cannot serve or if you are not married, the court uses its judgment—not yours—to choose someone.

Traditional Estate Planning Often Results in Probate

When you pass away owning property in your individual name, that property generally has to go through Probate before it can be distributed to your loved ones. And, very often, traditional estate planning leaves at least a portion of your property subject to Probate.

Probate is a court process, which means that it is public. It is also time-consuming. This means that your loved ones may not be able to access your property—sometimes for extended periods of time—as it makes its way through the process. Probate can also be expensive, meaning that property you'd intended to distribute to your loved ones might instead be used to pay court costs, legal fees, and other expenses associated with the Probate process.

Traditional Estate Planning Does Not Always Minimize Taxes

When your estate plan does not adequately anticipate the potential impact of gift, estate, or other taxes, you are likely sacrificing your ability to minimize or eliminate their impact. Traditional estate planning often fails to anticipate the potential impact of taxes and therefore exposes your estate to more tax liability than is necessary. This means that the federal and state governments can become unintended Beneficiaries of your estate.

Since tax laws are subject to change at any time, the government essentially has the power to intervene in your estate plan at will. All too often traditional estate planning is simply not equipped to anticipate these changes.

Traditional Estate Planning Does Not Always Look Far Enough Into the Future

One of the goals of estate planning is to leave the best possible inheritance and legacy for your spouse and children, and even for your grandchildren. Often, traditional estate plans simply dump money and other property directly on your loved ones and go no further. When this happens, property is left vulnerable to all kinds of threats.

For instance, if you leave property outright to your spouse, that property is vulnerable to the claims of your spouse's creditors. It is also vulnerable in the event that your spouse remarries and later divorces or predeceases his or her new spouse. Under this circumstance, the new spouse could walk away with a portion of the inheritance in the form of a divorce settlement or inheritance.

The same is true of inheritances that you leave outright to your children. Property distributed in this manner is left vulnerable in the event of a lawsuit, divorce, or to the negative consequences of a poor financial decision.

These are just a few of the ways in which traditional estate planning can fail to truly preserve your legacy—and to protect your loved ones' future. Let's now take a closer look at some of the problems associated with traditional estate planning.

Chapter 8
Someone to Watch Over Me: Living Probate

Each is the only safe guardian of his own rights and interests.
—John Stuart Mill

When you think of Probate, you think of something that happens when you die. Unfortunately, Probate can also happen while you're still alive. Often called *"Living Probate,"* the legal term for this process is a *"Guardianship"* or *"Conservatorship"* proceeding.

If you become mentally disabled during your lifetime, someone will need to step in and take care of your assets and your personal affairs. If no prior arrangements have been made, then your family will need to go to court to have someone appointed for the job. The person appointed by the court to manage your personal affairs is usually called a guardian. The person appointed to manage your assets is typically called a conservator.

The Living Probate Process

Just like the Probate process that takes place when a person passes away, the Living Probate process is controlled by state law. This means that the exact steps vary from state to state. However, the general process is much the same, no matter where you live. If you become mentally disabled without a plan for the management of your assets and your personal affairs, your family will need to go through these steps:

1. A close family member generally petitions the Probate court to be appointed guardian and/or conservator. This may involve hiring an attorney to file the appropriate paperwork, which must include

specific information as to why your family member believes you are mentally disabled.

2. Interested parties are notified.

3. A notice of hearing may need to be published.

4. A hearing is held during which the judge considers testimony, including the opinions of medical experts, as to whether or not you are able to manage your own affairs.

5. The judge decides whether or not to appoint a guardian and/or conservator.

6. Both guardians and conservators are accountable to the court, and remain under court oversight for as long as they remain in control of you or your assets.

Disadvantages of Living Probate

Living Probate carries with it a number of disadvantages.

First, it is a highly intrusive process under which you lose a great deal of privacy. Your personal financial and medical conditions are subject to the scrutiny of the court during a proceeding that can be open to the public—and advertised through a notice of hearing!

Second, you have no control over who is appointed to manage the most personal details of your life and your finances. Of course, it is the duty of the court to attempt to appoint a guardian or conservator who is fit and appropriate to serve in this capacity, but the judge who makes this decision will likely have no knowledge of you or your family. The person appointed may very well be the last person you would have chosen.

Third, the Living Probate process can be time-consuming and expensive. It takes time to compile the appropriate information, put it in the appropriate format, and file it with the court. It takes additional time to schedule the hearing and notify the appropriate parties. Of course, this doesn't account for the possibility of delays. And, as with any court proceeding, there are attorney's and expert's fees involved with the initial Guardianship or Conservatorship hearing, as well as the expenses involved in reporting to the court as the Guardianship or Conservatorship continues.

Traditional Estate Planning Is Not Very Effective for Avoiding Living Probate

The traditional estate planning methods discussed in the first section of this book have not proven very effective at avoiding Living Probate. Let's take a look at them one at a time.

The Will
A Will is powerless to help you avoid Living Probate because it takes effect only at the time of your death. Therefore, it cannot control events that happen during your lifetime.

Joint Tenancy
Joint Tenancy does nothing to avoid Living Probate. When property is owned in Joint Tenancy, both Joint Tenants must sign all documents relating to the property. This means that if one Joint Tenant becomes mentally disabled, Living Probate is required before any action can be taken with regard to the property.

Beneficiary Designations
When you designate a Beneficiary for a bank account, a life insurance policy, or another asset, this designation does not take effect until after your death. Beneficiary designations cannot control events that happen during your lifetime. Therefore, designating a Beneficiary does not help you avoid Living Probate.

The Basic Living Trust
Under certain circumstances, a traditional Living Trust might avoid Living Probate. In order for this to happen, the Trust has to have appropriate, up-to-date language that provides for management of the Trust assets in the event of your disability, and it has to be fully funded. This means that all the appropriate property must be transferred into the Trust. Any property left outside of your Trust will be out of your Trustee's reach and may be subject to Living Probate.

No Plan?
Lastly, having no plan in place guarantees you and your loved ones will have to endure the Living Probate process.

Chapter 9
Tied Up in Probate: Death Probate and Why Some Want to Avoid It

Let us endeavor to live so that when we die even the undertaker will be sorry.

—Mark Twain

Probate is the court-controlled process for distributing the assets titled in your name at the time of your death. Depending on the state, the size of your estate, your financial and tax status, and the complexity and cordiality of your family relationships, Probate has the potential to turn into a very time-consuming and expensive process.

Let's take a look at the basic steps involved in the Probate process:

Step One: The Probate Petition Is Filed

The Probate process begins when a formal written petition or application is filed in court, and the appropriate filing fee is paid. The probate court then officially appoints someone to represent your estate. If you died leaving behind a Will, the person you nominated to serve as Executor is normally appointed as the representative of your estate. If you died without a Will, the court is responsible for appointing an Administrator (usually a family member who requests the task) to handle the affairs of your estate. Some states, including Minnesota and North Dakota, use the blanket term *"Personal Representative"* to refer to either an Executor or an Administrator.

Your Personal Representative will most likely hire an attorney to help him or her navigate the legal and procedural requirements that come along with the Probate process. Once the probate petition is filed, a copy of it will be provided to the appropriate heirs and Beneficiaries of your estate.

Step Two: Your Creditors are Notified

Not only do the heirs and Beneficiaries who stand to inherit from your estate need to be notified that Probate is underway, but your creditors are also entitled to be notified so that they can present their claims to the court.

Before this can happen, your Personal Representative has to find and list all of your assets and liabilities. Then, your creditors are notified either by mail or through a notice published in the local newspaper. They are given a specific period of time to file their claims with the probate court, ordinarily a period of months.

Step Three: Your Assets are Inventoried and Appraised

In addition to listing your liabilities, your Personal Representative is responsible for making an inventory of your assets. He or she has to list all the items you own and ascertain the value of each item. There are a large number of items, such as real estate, antiques, motor vehicles, collectibles, and other valuables that require formal, written appraisals. These appraisals need to be done by professionals, and they cost money. The appraisal fees are paid from your estate, and paying these fees has the effect of depleting the assets left to distribute to your loved ones.

Step Four: Debts, Expenses, Taxes, and Claims are Settled

Once it is clear exactly what the assets of your estate are, any valid expenses, debts, and taxes can be paid.

In addition to creditors' claims, once must consider the possibility of nursing home costs and/or medical assistance recovery claims that are recoverable against the estate. Also, there are other expenses that are taken care of as part of the Probate process. These expenses include funeral bills, attorney's and appraiser's fees, your Personal Representative's fee, and other miscellaneous expenses.

Another type of claim that occasionally arises during the Probate process is a Will contest. Because Probate is a public process, and because your heirs and Beneficiaries are notified of the existence of a Probate case and provided with a copy of your Will, it is relatively simple for a disgruntled family member to join in the proceeding and attempt to gain a larger inheritance or to invalidate your Will altogether. If a Will contest occurs, it will have to be resolved before the Probate process can be finalized.

Finally, if your estate is subject to gift or estate taxes, the appropriate tax returns will have to be filed, the taxes paid, and confirmation received from the taxing authorities so that the estate can be closed.

Step Five: Final Distribution Is Made and Probate Is Closed

Once the probate court is satisfied that all the appropriate steps have been followed and all legal requirements have been met, it will order that the remaining assets be distributed to the appropriate heirs or Beneficiaries. If you passed away leaving behind a Will, the assets left over after Step Four will be distributed to the Beneficiaries named in your Will. If you passed away without a Will, your remaining assets will be distributed to your heirs, according to the provisions of state law. When this step is complete, the court closes your file, and the Probate process is complete.

The Disadvantages of Probate

There are a number of reasons some people wish to avoid Probate. These include:

1. **Expense.** Probate can be a costly undertaking. The expenses involved include attorneys' and appraisers' fees, court costs, and Personal Representatives' fees. Fees vary from state to state, but nationally, the average cost is between 2% and 5% of the gross value of the estate. For a married couple, if each spouse's estate is probated, Probate can be even more expensive, because much of the same property ends up being probated twice.

2. **Time.** Probate can be a time-consuming process. Some estates take months to make their way through the Probate process, while estates that involve family disputes or questions involving complex assets can take years. One of the biggest drawbacks to the process is that your assets are not always available to your loved ones while Probate is pending, hence the saying *"tied up in Probate."*

3. **Lack of Privacy.** Probate is a court proceeding, which means that it's public. If you have a Will, it is filed with the court at the start of the Probate process. Your Probate file includes an inventory and appraisal of every asset you owned at death. It also includes the names of your Beneficiaries and the amounts and conditions of their inheritances.

   Combine this with the fact that notice of the Probate proceeding is published in the local newspaper and anyone—from your nosy neighbor to individuals who may want to take advantage of your loved ones—can get access to your Probate file.

4. **The Opportunity for Will Contests and Other Trouble.** Since Probate is a public process, unscrupulous creditors can try to take advantage of your loved ones. There are those who file false claims against estates and those who attempt to convince family members that they are

personally responsible for a decedent's debts when this simply is not the case. Unfortunately, due to their emotional involvement and lack of knowledge about the Probate process, it can be easy for those close to you to be victimized.

Probate also makes it easier for unhappy family members to contest your Will. It is relatively easy to join a legal proceeding already in progress, and this is exactly what Probate is. So, whether or not their claim has merit, a disgruntled relative can bring a Will contest, causing both added expense and delay.

5. **The Potential for Multiple Probate Proceedings.** If you own property in more than one state, not only will Probate be necessary in your home state, it will also be necessary in each additional state in which your property is located. This means additional time, expense, and hassle for your loved ones.

6. **Emotional Cost.** Perhaps the biggest disadvantage to the Probate process is the emotional toll that it takes on your family. The process can drag on and be a constant reminder of grief and loss, causing stress that results in unnecessary conflict among loved ones.

Traditional Estate Planning Is Not Very Effective for Avoiding Probate

Just as the traditional estate planning methods discussed in the first section of this book have not proven very effective for avoiding Living Probate, they're not very effective for avoiding Death Probate, either. Let's take a look at them one at a time.

The Will

A Will does not help you avoid Probate. In fact, just the opposite is true. The word Probate actually means *"to prove a Will."* All property that is controlled by your Will is required to go through the Probate process before it can be distributed to your Beneficiaries.

Joint Tenancy

Joint Tenancy is only a partial solution to the problem of Probate. For example, when a husband and wife own property as Joint Tenants, the property passes outside of Probate when the first spouse dies. However, at the death of the second spouse, the property has to go through the Probate process. As a practical matter, owning property as Joint Tenants simply serves to delay the inevitable.

Beneficiary Designations

Assets for which you have designated a Beneficiary will pass outside of Probate. However, this is not an effective estate planning solution for at least two reasons. First, for most people, it is impossible to designate a Beneficiary for every single asset. This results in assets for which a Beneficiary has not been designated becoming subject to Probate. Second, if your spouse is your Beneficiary, the asset left to him or her is often subject to Probate upon his or her death.

The Basic Living Trust

The basic Living Trust avoids Probate in theory, but may fail to do so in practice. In order for this estate planning tool to be effective, it must be fully funded. This means that any asset that would otherwise be subject to Probate must be transferred into your Trust before you pass away. In reality, most basic Living Trusts remain unfunded or, at best, are only partially funded. This means that assets left out of the Trust are still in your individual name and are left to make their way through the Probate process.

Chapter 10
Who Gets Grandma's Pie Plate? Estate Disputes

When it comes time to divide an estate, the politest men quarrel.
—Ralph Waldo Emerson

Disputes over an estate can arise for the unlikeliest of reasons. It is not always the heirs of those who pass away leaving millions that end up battling in court for years. Even modest estates can spark Will contests and other litigation. For some families, the fights that never even see a courtroom can last the longest and cause the most damage.

Will Contests

When it comes to Will contests, there are the rules and theories that purport to govern how disagreements over Wills always turn out, and then there's the unfortunate reality that sometimes prevails. Let's look at both.

The Textbook Rules
State law controls who can file a Will contest and under what circumstances. In order to successfully challenge a Will, an individual or entity must have *"standing"* and must prove the appropriate grounds.

Who Has Standing to Contest a Will?
Only those who have *"standing,"* that is, those who will be personally affected by the outcome of the case, are legally permitted to file a lawsuit contesting a Will. In Minnesota and North Dakota, any *"interested person,"* as defined by statute, can begin an action to contest a Will. Those who have standing generally fall into three categories:

■ **Heirs at Law.** Your Heirs at Law are the relatives who would be entitled to inherit from you if you had no Will. For example, if you create a Will that disinherits your spouse or one of your children, or leaves one of these individuals less than they believe they're entitled to, they would have standing to challenge your Will. Whether or not they would win is a different question.

■ **Beneficiaries Named in a Prior Will.** A person or entity, like a charity, named in a previous Will, but omitted or disinherited in your current Will, might have standing to challenge your current Will. The same is true for a Beneficiary who receives a reduced share in your current Will.

■ **Creditors**

What Are the Grounds for a Will Contest?
The grounds for a Will contest fall into four general categories.

1. **Improper Execution.** In order to be valid, a Will must be in writing, and it must be properly signed and witnessed. Each state has specific laws that control how a Will is to be signed, how many witnesses are required, and who those witnesses must be. The most common reason that Wills are contested—and that Wills are found to be invalid—is failure to sign a Will in accordance with state law.

2. **Lack of Testamentary Capacity.** Will cannot be valid unless the person making it is of legal age and is mentally competent at the time the Will is signed. This is known as having *"testamentary capacity."* What determines whether a person has testamentary capacity? He or she must:

   ■ *Know that he or she is creating a Will*

   ■ *Know the nature and value of his or her property*

   ■ *Know who would ordinarily inherit that property*

■ *Understand the legal effect of making a Will*

If an heir or Beneficiary contests your Will on the basis of lack of testamentary capacity, witnesses will need to testify concerning their observations of your behavior around the time you made your Will. These witnesses might include experts, such as your doctor, or family members and friends, or they might include your estate planning attorney or the actual witnesses to your Will. The key to proving your lack of testamentary capacity lies in their ability to provide evidence showing that you did not understand the significance of your actions in making your Will.

3. **Undue Influence or Duress.** You know the scenario: The elderly father changes his Will during the last days of his life, leaving the bulk of his fortune to one of his two sons and leaving his other son a mere pittance. Was this a conscious choice on the part of the father, or did the now-wealthy son exert undue influence over his dad, causing him to make a change he really didn't intend?

In a case of undue influence, one Beneficiary of your estate exerts inappropriate pressure on you to give him or her a disproportionate share of your estate. In this type of Will contest, the heir or Beneficiary challenging your Will would need to show that:

■ *Undue influence was exercised on you.*

■ *The effect of that influence was to overpower your mind and take away your free will.*

■ *The result was that you created a Will that does not reflect your wishes, but, rather, reflects the wishes of the Beneficiary who exerted the undue influence.*

■ *The provisions of your Will would have been different, had it not been for the exercise of undue influence.*

In a case of duress, the maker of the Will is inappropriately pressured through the use of threats or the performance of wrongful acts, which results in a Will that does not match the true intent of the individual.

4. **Fraud.** When an heir or Beneficiary challenges your Will on the basis of fraud, he or she must prove that you were tricked into signing it. When your Will is procured by fraud, it means that you sign it thinking that it is another type of document, such as a deed or a Power of Attorney.

The Unfortunate Reality
A Will, by its very nature, must be probated. Probate, as a public, court-administered process, can encourage contesting of a Will. Public notice is sent to creditors, letting them know they have a limited time within which to bring a claim against your estate. This notice is apt to attract the attention of others who might feel they can lay claim to a part of your estate, legitimate or not. It is relatively easy for an interested party to join in routine probate court proceedings already in progress and contest the Will.

The immediate effect of estate litigation, whether that litigation is frivolous or legitimate, is to put a hold on the assets in question, so that your loved ones cannot access them while the dispute is pending. In the face of a potentially expensive and time-consuming court battle, it can be easy for your Personal Representative or your heirs to settle with the person contesting your Will, whether the claim is legitimate or not.

What About Basic Living Trusts?

Since assets funded into a Trust do not go through Probate, there are typically no court proceedings involved in the administration of your Trust, and there is no public notice that your Trust is being administered. These facts make it less likely that a lawsuit will be filed contesting your

Trust. However, as we have seen, one of the most common problems with a Basic Living Trust is that often the Trust is either completely unfunded or significant assets are left out of the Trust.

This means that these assets are subject to Probate, which can invite litigation. Therefore, even with a Basic Living Trust, the threat of estate litigation is still a possibility.

Fights Outside of Court

Often, the most intense disagreements when it comes to a loved one's estate arise over assets that don't have much monetary value and may not even fall under the authority of a probate judge. Many probate attorneys can tell you stories about families that were nearly torn apart by fights over who would keep Dad's pipe collection or Grandma's pie plate.

These are exactly the types of assets that tend to fall through the cracks when it comes to traditional estate planning. The result is that cherished items that could be the source of warm memories instead become the cause of bitter and enduring family discord.

Chapter 11

Running Toward a Moving Target: The Estate Tax

The wisdom of man never yet contrived a system of taxation that would operate with perfect equality.

—Andrew Jackson

Are you rich? You might be quick to answer *"no"* to this question. Yet often, people are surprised to find out that they are, in fact, *"wealthy"* in the eyes of the IRS even when they don't see themselves as particularly *"wealthy"* by everyday standards.

The Federal Estate Tax

When you pass away, the IRS adds up everything you own for the purpose of determining whether or not your estate will be subject to the federal estate tax. In other words, the IRS determines whether, by its standards, you are *"wealthy."* The property considered by the IRS includes assets such as:

- Real estate, including your family home

- Cash

- Stocks and bonds

- Life insurance

- Personal property, including furniture, artwork, electronics, tools, etc.

- Retirement accounts and other financial accounts

What Is the Estate Tax and Who Avoids It?

The estate tax is a tax that is levied on your right to transfer property at death. Not every estate is subject to the estate tax, which is one of the reasons the IRS calculates the exact value of your estate at the time of your death. There are actually two groups of people who automatically avoid the tax.

1. **Those Who Fall Under the Estate Tax Exclusion.** Each individual is allowed to pass on a certain amount of wealth at death without triggering the estate tax. This is called the Estate Tax Exclusion, and the exact dollar amount of the exclusion is set by Congress. Because of this, the exclusion has the potential to vary from year to year as Congress enacts new estate tax legislation. If the value of your estate, as totaled by the IRS, is larger than the Estate Tax Exclusion in effect during the year of your death, and your estate does not fall under any other exceptions that would reduce or eliminate your estate tax obligation, then you'll pay tax at the rate in effect at that time.

Married Couples. Married couples get an additional, albeit temporary, estate tax break in the form of the Unlimited Marital Deduction. If you're married, you can pass your whole estate—regardless of its size—to your spouse without paying any estate tax at the time of your death. This is only a temporary tax break, though, because your assets become part of your spouse's estate. Later, when he or she passes away, any amount of your spouse's estate that exceeds the effective Estate Tax Exclusion will be subject to taxation. Under the tax law, ATRA 2012, a feature known as a *"portability election"* was made permanent. In many situations, a surviving spouse may elect portability and apply to have the decedent's unused exclusion amount be added to the surviving spouse's transfers during life and death.

State Estate Taxes

Many states impose their own estate tax in addition to the federal estate tax. Each state sets its own Estate Tax Exclusion amount and tax rate, and their estate tax laws may differ quite a bit from the federal law. For individuals who reside in these states, or even own property there, the result can be a large tax bill when it comes time to settle an estate. Minnesota is one of those states that sets its own state estate tax. Given the dynamic changes in both the federal and Minnesota estate taxes, it is important to involve a qualified estate planning attorney and/or a tax professional.

Traditional Estate Planning Falls Short When It Comes to Minimizing Estate Taxes

The problem with traditional estate planning—including simple Wills, unfunded and partially funded Basic Living Trusts, and, of course, failure to plan altogether—is that these methods expose your estate to the greatest degree of taxation. This is certainly true when it comes to federal estate taxes, and, depending on where you live and where you own property, it may also be true when it comes to the taxes levied by your state government when you pass away.

These traditional estate planning methods fall short because they leave your estate at the mercy of the government when there are alternatives that can minimize or even eliminate your estate tax bill, preserving more of your wealth for your loved ones.

Chapter 12
Prying Eyes: Probate and Privacy

Privacy is not something that I'm merely entitled to, it's an absolute prerequisite.

—Marlon Brando

Do you make your family finances a regular topic of conversation with your neighbors? What about custody arrangements for your children— do all the teachers at school know the ins and outs of your agreement with your former spouse? Would you rush to share all the inner workings of your family business with your top competitors? Of course not!

Probate Is a Public Process

Anyone who is so inclined can walk into the local courthouse, look through a probate file, and find just this type of personal information at his or her fingertips. There's no permission necessary, and no one will raise an eyebrow.

If you pass away leaving property that is subject to Probate, notice of your probate proceedings will normally be published in a general circulation newspaper in your community. As you likely know, local newspapers aren't strictly local anymore; many of them are published online as well as in print.

Your Probate File Discloses Personal Information

This can put the spotlight on your probate file, which will:

- Disclose an inventory and appraisal of every asset you owned at the time of your death

- Reveal the names of all your creditors and the amount you owed to each

- State the names of each and every one of your Beneficiaries, along with the amounts and conditions of their inheritances

If you own a business, your probate file may further disclose sensitive information about the assets and liabilities of your company and the manner in which control of your business will transition.

Lack of Privacy Can Leave Your Loved Ones Vulnerable

This disclosure puts information you might prefer not to share in the hands of anyone who's interested, from the neighborhood gossip to your business competitors.

It also puts your loved ones at the mercy of a range of predators, including unscrupulous creditors. Some may try to convince your grieving heirs that they are personally liable for debts you may or may not have owed, but that your loved ones are not responsible for paying in any case.

The public nature of the probate process has even spawned an entire industry of *"probate investors"* who target probate files and search for property to buy at a heavy discount.

Lack of privacy is one of the primary disadvantages of the probate system. One of the failings of traditional estate planning is that the methods it employs tend to leave at least a portion of your assets subject to Probate, and therefore open to prying eyes.

Chapter 13

Pay No Attention to the Man Behind the Curtain: Intervention in Your Family's Affairs

A clear vision, backed by definite plans, gives you a tremendous feeling of confidence and personal power.

—Brian Tracy

One of the primary reasons that people plan their estates is to ensure that their property makes its way into the hands of those they hold most dear. Another primary reason for estate planning is to provide for the well-being of young children in the event of your untimely death. If you are the parent of young children, or if you are not married to your partner, you have special and unique concerns when it comes to creating your estate plan.

Unfortunately, an inadequate estate plan can have the biggest impact on people in these two situations. Without comprehensive planning, the state decides what will happen to your children and your property, and the results can be far different from what you would have wanted.

Concerns for Parents of Young Children

If you are the parent of young children, one of your primary estate planning goals is most likely to provide for your children's future well-being and financial security. You might be surprised to find that traditional estate planning methods fall short when it comes to making sure that your wishes concerning your children are communicated and honored. In the event that both you and your children's other parent pass away before your children reach adulthood, your children's futures may be left in the hands of a well-meaning but possibly ill-informed judge. Making sure your minor children are taken care of in the event of your death requires two separate components: the physical care of your children and the management of your children's finances.

Who Will Take Care of Your Children If You Can't Be There?
If your children are left without parents before they reach the *"age of majority"* (eighteen in most states, including Minnesota and North Dakota), they will need a guardian. A guardian is a legally-appointed adult who is responsible for taking care of your children's needs. The guardian would be in charge of providing food, clothing, and housing for your children, making decisions concerning your children's education, and otherwise guiding your children into adulthood, making sure that they're safe and protected.

This is one area of estate planning where a Will is absolutely essential. Although, as we've seen, a Will is not effective as a stand-alone estate plan, if you pass away leaving a Will that names a guardian for your children, assuming the children's other parent does not survive you, the court normally appoints whomever you've nominated as guardian. The only reason the nominated guardian would not be appointed for the job would be if the court finds that it is not in your children's best interest for him or her to serve.

What if your Will nominates a guardian who cannot serve when the time comes, or what if you die leaving behind no Will?

In this situation, the state decides who will bring up your children. This means that the court will hold a hearing, and a judge will appoint someone to serve as guardian. Generally, the judge chooses from among any relatives or other individuals who have petitioned the court for the role. While the judge will act in good faith, with the goal of appointing a guardian who will serve the best interests of your children, he or she will not know anything about you or your family. He or she will have little to no knowledge of your beliefs and values, your views on education, the rules and routines your children have been brought up with, or any of the little details about your family that would truly enable him or her to make the best possible decision for your children.

Who Will Manage Your Children's Money in Your Absence?

Just as your minor children can't be left to raise themselves in your absence, they also can't be left to manage their own money and other property. Unless you've made other legally-effective provisions for the management of your children's money, the court will appoint a conservator to manage any money or property your children inherit.

The process for appointing a conservator is similar to the process for appointing a guardian, and the court's role is to do the best it can to act in the best interests of your children. In many cases, the person who has been named your children's guardian will also be named conservator of their assets, although sometimes the guardian and conservator are two different people.

A court-supervised Conservatorship has a number of disadvantages, not the least of which is that, as a rule, your beliefs, values, and wishes do not factor into the financial decisions that are made on behalf of your children.

1. Your children's inheritance is subject to court oversight and scrutiny. At first blush, this might not seem like a disadvantage. After all, isn't it comforting to think that the court will ensure that your children's conservator does not make unscrupulous decisions when it comes to your children's inheritance? The problem is that the court oversight involved in a Conservatorship is a one-size-fits all arrangement. For example, it doesn't make allowances for a scenario under which the guardian nominated in your Will has also been appointed to manage your children's money, and you have full trust and confidence in this person's ability to do the job.

Conservatorship places some pretty serious restrictions on your children's inheritance, such as:

- *Putting your children's money into accounts for which the conservator has little or no control over investment decisions*

- *Requiring the conservator to obtain the Judge's approval before making a range of decisions that involve spending money on your children*

- *Obligating the conservator to make an annual accounting to the court. This means that, each year, the conservator must prepare a written report of income and expenses and present it to the Judge for approval. Often, the help of an accountant or attorney is needed, and the fees for these services come out of your children's inheritance.*

2. Each child's inheritance is turned over to him or her when they reach the *"age of majority."* In most states, including Minnesota and North Dakota, this is age eighteen. Especially if your children stand to inherit a sizable amount of money or property, this thought might make you shudder. Very few individuals of their age are mature or responsible enough to make the wise financial decisions you'd want them to make. However, Conservatorship, as a one-size-fits-all option, does not take into account a child's maturity level, personality, or life experience when it comes to handing over an inheritance.

3. The arrangement does not allow you to choose:

- *Who will manage your children's money*

- *The age at which money is distributed to your children*

- *How exactly your children's inheritance is spent*

Traditional estate planning often leaves gaps that subject your children's inheritance to a court-appointed Conservatorship. The tragic potential result is a financial future that is much less bright than it could have otherwise been.

Concerns for Unmarried Couples

If you and your partner are not married, then you are especially vulnerable when it comes to the issues that surround estate planning. No matter how long and committed your relationship, whether you are in a same-sex or heterosexual relationship, you simply don't enjoy the same rights as married couples. What does this mean from an estate planning perspective?

What Happens to Your Partner's Inheritance?
Without an effective estate plan, you are vulnerable to the intestacy laws of your state. These are the default rules for determining how property is distributed at death, and they are based on traditional ideas of family. This means that, absent effective estate planning, in the eyes of the law, your partner will be treated as a stranger to you when you pass away. Your property may go to your nearest living relatives, as defined by the law of the state in which you reside. Generally, this means your property will be distributed to your children, your parents, your siblings, or some combination of these blood relatives.

No Estate Plan
Without an estate plan, your partner will not be entitled to any portion of your property that is subject to Probate.

Basic Living Trust
If you leave behind a Living Trust that is not fully funded at the time of your death, then your partner runs the risk of being disinherited when it comes to any assets not transferred into the Trust.

Joint Tenancy

Any property you and your partner co-own as Joint Tenants with Rights of Survivorship will pass to your partner outside of Probate in the event of your death. However, as we have seen, Joint Tenancy carries with it a number of disadvantages, including potential negative tax consequences. Further, it is impractical if not impossible to attempt to own every single asset in Joint Tenancy.

Will

While a Will can be an effective means of transferring your property to your partner upon your death, it is not effective for incapacity planning purposes, and it has to be probated. This carries with it certain drawbacks that are of particular concern to unmarried partners. For instance:

- The probate process has the potential to invite a Will contest. Parents or other family members who may not approve of your life choices can contest your Will. Even if they're not successful in having your Will invalidated, they can succeed in tying up your estate, increasing legal fees, and making your grieving partner even more miserable.

- Probate exposes your personal relationship to the public.

What about Domestic Partnership?

If your state allows registration as domestic partners, taking this step may offer you some degree of protection when it comes to intestacy laws (dying without an estate plan). However, even then, you have no real control over the distribution of your assets, and the state's plan for who gets your property and the amount given to each individual during the probate process might not meet your expectations.

What Happens If You Become Disabled?

All of us are vulnerable to accidents and illnesses that, at any time, could render us unable to care for ourselves, make financial decisions, or even tell our doctors what medical treatments we do and don't want. Unfortunately, in the eyes of the law, your unmarried partner is seldom the first choice to be given the authority to step in and make these decisions on your behalf.

As we have seen, traditional estate planning methods tend to fall short when it comes to putting in place an effective disability plan. Without an effective plan, your partner may not have the right to access your healthcare information, let alone make medical decisions for you. In fact, he or she may not even be allowed to visit you in the hospital.

Traditional estate planning simply does not cover all the bases when it comes to protecting unmarried partners.

Chapter 14
Creditors and Predators

Misery is the company of lawsuits.

—Francois Rabelais

Most traditional estate planning methods leave your assets to your spouse and children *"outright,"* meaning that each of your Beneficiaries gets his or her inheritance in one lump sum. This is a big problem if you want to protect your spouse and adult children from the threat of lawsuits, scams, and other situations that can dissipate their inheritances and destroy your financial legacy.

Lawsuits

You may wonder what your spouse or children could ever do to get themselves sued. The brief answer is that everyone makes mistakes or uses poor judgment on occasion. One moment's lapse in attention can result in a car accident with an accompanying lawsuit. Or, your spouse or child could get behind on paying his or her bills and be sued by a creditor.

Even if your loved ones don't make mistakes, they can still be vulnerable to frivolous lawsuits. The harsh reality is that we live in a litigious society, where people are looking for someone to hold accountable for their difficulties or their own poor decisions. A simple fender bender or a tree limb falling on a neighbor's home can start a lawsuit that has the potential to ruin your loved ones financially.

How can a lawsuit result in the loss of an inheritance? Let's look at an example:

Don passes away, leaving his share of their assets to his wife, Joan. Because Don and Joan had a traditional estate plan, there was no built-in lawsuit protection. Instead, Joan inherited Don's assets outright, in one lump sum.

One day, Joan is driving to her daughter's house to visit the grandchildren. She takes her eyes off the road for just a moment and runs into a school bus filled with children. There are some serious injuries, and Joan finds herself being sued. The trial ends with a $2 million judgment against Joan—far more than her car insurance will cover.

Because Don left all of his assets directly to Joan, those assets are combined with hers and can be collected in payment of the judgment, spelling financial disaster for Joan.

Scams

When your spouse or children receive an inheritance in one lump sum that's distributed directly to them, that inheritance can also be vulnerable to scam artists and other predators.

Just as there are individuals who scour the probate records looking for estate assets to buy out from under your loved ones, there are also those who use the same records to find people who have recently inherited large sums of money. They then contact the unsuspecting Beneficiaries and offer them foolish financial investments or get-rich-quick schemes.

Beyond this, there are countless scam artists who seek to steal money, often targeting older individuals. While some of these scams can be spotted a mile away, others are well-planned and have the potential to deceive even the most alert among us. For instance, a recent scam added a new twist on an old theme. Here's how it works:

Most of us have heard about the telephone scam where a thief will call a grandparent, posing as that person's grandchild. The *"grandchild"* has gotten into some minor legal trouble, or has had a car accident, and needs help in the form of some emergency cash. The unsuspecting grandparent wires the requested funds, which are never seen again.

People began to get wise to this scam and started asking personal questions to verify the caller's identity. For instance, grandparents were instructed to ask the name of a childhood pet, or where the *"grandchild"* attended school.

The ever-crafty scammers have begun using the real grandchild's social media pages in order to correctly answer these personal questions and fool the diligent grandparent.

When it comes to protecting your spouse, children, and grandchildren from scams and fraud, traditional estate planning methods again fall short. When your loved ones inherit money outright, that money is not protected from those who would seek to take advantage of them.

Protecting Your Loved Ones from Themselves

Particularly when it comes to inheritances for adult children or grandchildren, there is another reason that passing on money or property outright might be a bad idea. You've spent a lifetime building wealth, and that work can go up in smoke in a matter of months if it's distributed to a loved one who has a substance abuse problem, or who is simply not ready for that wealth. There are countless stories of children who have wasted an inheritance on expensive cars, clothes, and vacations, or lost their parents' hard-earned wealth through poor decision-making. Consider the case of Alan:

Alan is not quite 30 years old and he's never been very good with money. Perhaps that is why he's never had much money before. He's just come into an inheritance of $500,000, free and clear. What is the first thing he does? He goes shopping for a new car; not just any car, but the ultimate American Muscle car, the Corvette. He walks into the dealership with cash and picks out the newest and fastest model that goes from 0 to 60 in 4.2 seconds. He is extremely proud of his new toy and finds every occasion to race it.

Fortunately, he doesn't get into a car accident, but he does get a rude awakening from the IRS. When it comes to money, Alan has never been terribly responsible. Apparently, he has failed to file tax returns for the past several years. With interest and penalties, his tax bill adds up to more than $75,000. As you might expect, the IRS walks in and scoops up the money right out of John's bank account. The traditional estate plan provided no protection for Alan. In addition to the negative consequences of his spendthrift actions, he is left wide open and exposed to lawsuits and creditor claims.

Traditional estate planning does not do enough to protect your spouse and children from outside forces and real life situations that threaten their inheritances. Even worse, in some circumstances, it does not do enough to protect your loved ones from themselves.

Chapter 15
After the I Do's: Remarriage and Divorce

Love, the quest; marriage, the conquest; divorce, the inquest.
—**Helen Rowland**

Just as traditional estate planning fails to protect your spouse and children from lawsuits and scams, it also fails to protect their inheritances from disappearing because of remarriage or divorce.

Remarriage

Imagine you've passed away and, eventually, your spouse decides to remarry. You've left your property to your spouse under a traditional estate plan, so it remains unshielded. Presumably, you want your spouse to have the use of this property during his or her lifetime, and then you want him or her to pass that property on to your children. There's a good chance that the property you passed on will never make it into the hands of your children. Let's look at three scenarios:

1. Your wife remarries, and her new husband has children of his own. Knowing that you've left your wife a significant amount of property, and that she now owns this property outright, the new husband and/ or his children convince your wife to sign over title to significant portions of her assets. After all, they are in love and now a family, right? The result? By the time your wife passes away, there is little or nothing left to hand down to your children, and the new husband and his children walk away with what you'd intended to be your kids' inheritance.

2. Your wife remarries, and her new husband has children of his own. They have a wonderful relationship, and he would never dream of taking advantage of her. Yet, if your wife passes away without an adequate estate plan, a sizable share of the property you passed on to her could go straight to her new husband under state intestacy laws. The intentions were entirely honorable, but the result is the same: your children's inheritance ends up in the hands of someone else's family.

3. Your wife remarries and, as with many American marriages today, things just don't work out. Eventually, she and her new husband part ways. Unfortunately, during the marriage, much of the property you left was placed into joint accounts or used to purchase property held by the couple as Joint Tenants With Rights of Survivorship. As part of the divorce, the new husband gets a share of your wife's property, including property that you'd intended for her to pass on to your children.

Each of these three scenarios is fairly common, and there are ways to plan around them to protect your spouse's estate and the inheritances of your children. Unfortunately, most traditional estate plans simply do not include the protections that are necessary to preserve your estate in these situations.

Divorce

With the divorce rate hovering around 50%, it is highly likely that one of your children or grandchildren will experience this unpleasant reality. When your child or grandchild receives an inheritance and then is a party to a subsequent divorce, that inheritance is at risk of being included in a divorce settlement. In some states, especially if funds are commingled, a divorcing spouse can walk away with half of the inheritance you leave your son, daughter, or grandchild if that inheritance is not protected.

Let's look at an example:

Your daughter, Jenny, is married with three children. You adore your daughter and your grandchildren, but you've never been crazy about Jack, Jenny's husband. He's bounced from one low-paying job to another and has never been terribly ambitious, leaving Jenny to serve as the main breadwinner for the family. When you and your spouse pass away, your estate plan leaves $500,000 to Jenny in one lump sum.

When Jenny receives her inheritance, she deposits the money into joint accounts with Jack. A few years later, when the couple decides that things just aren't going to work out, what happens? Jack walks away from the divorce with half of the money that was deposited into those joint accounts, and Jenny's inheritance, your life's work, is suddenly cut in half.

There are methods for protecting your children's and grandchildren's inheritances from the unpleasant realities of divorce. Unfortunately, traditional estate plans generally do not take this situation into account, leaving the potential for your hard-earned wealth to make its way into the hands of a former spouse who will soon be long gone.

Chapter 16

You Can't Take It With You: Retirement Planning and Your Beneficiaries

You must pay taxes. But there's no law that says you gotta leave a tip.
—**Advertisement**

If you are like many Americans, you likely have a Qualified Retirement Plan, such as a 401(k) or an IRA. The primary goal in having such a Retirement Plan is, of course, to provide you with income after you've left the workforce. However, Retirement Plans can be yet another way to leave an inheritance to your spouse, children, or grandchildren.

Traditional estate planning can place limits on the benefits your Retirement Plan can offer to your Beneficiaries. First, it often ignores the power of the Qualified Retirement Plan as an estate planning tool. Second, even when Plans such as IRA's and 401(k)'s are used for estate planning purposes, traditional estate planning methods often fall short when it comes to allowing your Beneficiaries to maximize the financial benefits they get from your retirement savings. Finally, traditional estate planning often fails to protect your Beneficiaries from creditors, predators, and IRS requirements.

How Do Qualified Retirement Plans Work?

A Qualified Retirement Plan is one that meets certain requirements of the Internal Revenue Code and is therefore eligible for special tax treatment.

Tax-Deferred Growth

When you contribute money to your traditional 401(k), IRA, or other Qualified Retirement Plan, that contribution is tax-deferred. Your contributions are made with pre-tax dollars, meaning that you don't pay any income tax on money going into the Plan. If you make a $1,000 contribution, it's as though you made $1,000 less income that year, reducing your tax bill.

Required Minimum Distributions

Your contributions are also allowed to grow without being taxed until you withdraw money from the Plan. The moment you take money out of your Qualified Retirement Plan, it is subject to income tax. This raises the question; why not just leave your money in a Qualified Retirement Plan forever, so that it can continue to grow indefinitely? There are two answers to this question:

1. Most of us contribute to a Qualified Retirement Plan because we'll actually need to use at least a portion of the funds in that Plan as income during retirement.

2. The IRS won't allow money to grow, tax-free, indefinitely. It wants its share of your money eventually, and it has established rules to ensure that, at some point, income tax is paid on the funds in a Qualified Retirement Plan.

During your lifetime, the IRS requires that you begin withdrawing a certain amount from your Plan on an annual basis beginning at age 70 ½. This is called a Required Minimum Distribution. The exact amount you're required to withdraw each year varies, and it is determined by your remaining life expectancy as well as the amount of funds in your Plan.

Beneficiaries and Required Minimum Distributions

For any money that is left in your Qualified Retirement Plan when you pass away, you're permitted to designate one or more Beneficiaries. When this person withdraws money from the Plan, he or she will be responsible for the accompanying income taxes, and, like you, he or she will be subject to a Required Minimum Distribution. The amount your Beneficiary is required to withdraw each year is based on his or her life expectancy as well as the balance of funds in the Retirement Plan. Your choice of Beneficiary determines when that Beneficiary's money must be taken out of the inherited Retirement Plan. The older the Beneficiary, the sooner funds must be withdrawn from the Plan, reducing its overall value to your Beneficiary.

Why Not Leave the Account Directly to a Beneficiary?

There are several problems with leaving a Qualified Retirement Plan directly to a Beneficiary, such as:

The Possibility of a Lump Sum Distribution

Once your Beneficiary inherits the account, he or she can decide not to take the Required Minimum Distribution from the account on an annual basis. Instead, he or she has every right to take one lump sum distribution of all the funds in the account. This can be a disastrous decision.

Any withdrawal from a Qualified Retirement Plan is taxable in the year it is taken. So, the decision to withdraw a large amount from the account will result in a hefty chunk of those funds being eaten up by income tax. In addition, one of the primary benefits of a Qualified Retirement Plan is its tax-deferred status. Even after a Beneficiary has inherited your account, the funds that remain in that account can continue to grow without being taxed. Taking a large distribution of funds eliminates this tax-deferred growth, effectively reducing the amount of your Beneficiary's inheritance.

Vulnerability to Creditors and Predators

As we have already seen, once money makes its way free and clear into the hands of your Beneficiary, it is unprotected. Leaving your Qualified

Retirement Plan to a loved one means that his or her inheritance becomes vulnerable to creditors, to a divorcing spouse, to those who might want to take advantage of your loved one, or to his or her own poor spending decisions and financial missteps.

Estate Taxes

Leaving your Qualified Retirement Plan outright to a Beneficiary does not allow for estate tax planning. This can be a special concern when it comes to leaving your Retirement Plan to your spouse. The inherited funds become part of his or her estate for estate tax purposes, possibly subjecting your spouse's estate to taxes and depleting the inheritance he or she is able to pass on to remaining loved ones.

Designating a Beneficiary for your Qualified Retirement Plan leaves you powerless to control the income and estate tax consequences, and it leaves your Beneficiary's inheritance vulnerable to a range of threats.

What About a Living Trust?

What about naming a basic Living Trust as Beneficiary of your Qualified Retirement Plan? There are a couple of potential problems with this approach.

Not all basic Living Trusts contain appropriate Retirement Plan language. In this situation, when you pass away, your Trustee is left without the ability to deal with your retirement accounts. The result is negative income tax consequences, including a reduced amount of time over which your Beneficiary is allowed to take Required Minimum Distributions from the account. This does away with the benefit of tax-deferred growth and has the unwanted effect of limiting your loved one's inheritance.

Even if your Living Trust has language concerning your Retirement Plan, it is important to consider who the Beneficiaries of the Trust are. If you designate more than one Trust Beneficiary, the IRS will use the oldest Beneficiary of the Trust as its measuring stick for the timing and amounts of Required Minimum Distributions.

Let's look at an example: You leave your Qualified Retirement Plan to your children and your mother. Your mother, at age 90, has a short life expectancy. Your children, on the other hand, are in their twenties with long life expectancies. Who do you think the IRS will consider the *"Beneficiary"*? Your mother, of course. She is the oldest Beneficiary, so the Required Minimum Distributions will be based on her remaining life expectancy. The result is that the funds in the Plan are withdrawn earlier and are therefore taxed sooner and depleted faster.

There are methods for protecting the retirement funds you pass on to your Beneficiaries, while at the same time ensuring that your Beneficiaries get the maximum tax deferral benefits. However, traditional estate plans, including basic Living Trusts, do not offer these protections.

Chapter 17

Mom Wanted Me to Have That!

It has long been an axiom of mine that the little things are infinitely the most important.

—Arthur Conan Doyle

What are your most treasured possessions? For many of us, the things that are most important are not necessarily those with the highest fair market value. Instead, our most valued possessions tend to be those to which we have an emotional attachment. Your most prized possession might be a pocket watch your grandfather handed down to you or a gift given to you by your spouse or child.

Traditional estate planning methods are designed with an eye toward distributing your financial assets to your loved ones when you pass away. Unfortunately, this often results in an estate plan that ignores or glosses over the issue of what will happen to your precious family heirlooms and other personal belongings at your death.

Why is the distribution of personal belongings an issue that is marginalized or even completely neglected by many traditional estate plans? One reason is that personal possessions often have less monetary value than the financial assets, so they're easy to ignore. Another reason is that the number of personal possessions owned by the average person can make it unwieldy at best to try to account for and fairly distribute each item using traditional estate planning tools.

Traditional estate planning often takes an approach that underestimates the emotional ties connecting your loved ones to your property. These emotional ties, combined with the often complex relationships that exist between family members, can amount to a powder keg when it comes to finalizing your estate.

Beyond the emotional ties certain family members might have to specific items of property, it is also common for conflict over personal property to stem from family members' misunderstandings as to the actual market value of that property. While Dad may have spent a small fortune on that camera or his vast array of tools, or everyone expected Uncle John's stamp collection to be worth thousands of dollars, these items might actually have little or no monetary value when the time comes to distribute property. Leaving grieving family members to divide personal possessions among them, especially when those family members may not understand the harsh reality concerning the actual value of certain items, can cause emotions to run high and invite conflict.

Traditional Approaches

It would be easy to solve the problem of how to distribute personal possessions if we could simply use a Will to spell out exactly who gets what. For the vast majority of us, though, this approach is just not practical. For one thing, most of us have far too many possessions to itemize each of them in a Will. More importantly, if we took this approach, we would have to make a new Will every time we bought or sold one of our possessions.

Some Wills and Living Trusts allow the Personal Representative or Trustee to distribute personal property as they, in their discretion, see fit. This approach can put an unfair burden on the Personal Representative or Trustee, placing him or her in a very uncomfortable position. It can also invite squabbles between family members.

Still other estate plans designate an order in which loved ones will be allowed to pick items of personal property to keep. This results in a rotation under which each Beneficiary chooses a single item of a decedent's property, and the selection continues until all the property in question is chosen. This approach also opens the door for fights and resentment among family members.

These options commonly used in traditional estate planning methods have a common denominator: They leave your loved ones with little or no guidance as to your wishes for who should receive what and when. This, in turn, invites conflict as various loved ones make their best guess as to what your intentions must have been.

Chapter 18
Gone But Not Forgotten?

We forget all too soon the things we thought we could never forget. We forget the loves and the betrayals alike, forget what we whispered and what we screamed, forget who we were.

—Joan Didion

Do you recall the mix of emotions you experienced when the time came to leave home and go to college or during your first year of marriage? How did you feel the first time you gazed into your newborn's eyes or, a few years later, when you were the one sending your *"baby"* off to college? If you've lost a loved one, what did your thoughts and concerns center on at that difficult time in your life?

Defining Moments

All of these times in our lives are defining moments; they are precious events that serve as emotional anchors for each of us. Life is never quite the same after a defining moment. One common and interesting thing is that when these moments happen, the last thing we are concerned about is the condition of our finances. Certainly, when we experience the loss of a loved one, we think about what they meant to our family and all the memories we have with that person. We cling to the things that made our loved one who they were, the stories, the values, the life lessons, and even their favorite sayings.

A Financial Inheritance Pales in Comparison to a Non-Financial Legacy

The Allianz American Legacies Study found that baby boomers and their parents rate the non-financial legacy you leave behind—your wisdom, life lessons, stories, morals, values, and faith—as ten times more important than a financial inheritance. Paradoxically, a traditional estate plan does nothing to preserve your non-financial legacy. A Will or a barebones Living Trust may do a passable job of ensuring that your real estate, investments, and financial accounts are distributed to your intended Beneficiaries, but it cannot give your children or grandchildren a sense of who you were, the values and life events that shaped you as a person, or your aspirations for those you leave behind.

What Will They Miss Most When You're Gone?

It is just these types of things that those who were closest to you will miss the most when you're gone. It is also exactly these things that future generations—the grandchildren and great-grandchildren who may not get to know you in person—stand to miss out on entirely. The sad thing is that it is possible to preserve the most important part of your legacy for your loved ones and for future generations, but for countless individuals who opt for traditional estate planning methods, this opportunity is regrettably lost. The result is the core of who they were, what they meant to the people around them, and what they wanted for those they held most dear is likely to be lost.

The remainder of this book is devoted to explaining how you can take a holistic view of wealth and estate planning through a concept called Legacy Wealth Planning. As you will see, this approach allows you to not only take on the important tasks of building, protecting, and passing on your financial wealth, it also allows you to engage in the essential work of leaving a non-financial legacy. By passing on a legacy in addition to an estate, you can help ensure that your children and grandchildren are financially secure and pass on the knowledge of who you are as a person: your hopes, your dreams and expectations for loved ones, and a sense of your family history, heritage, and belonging that otherwise might pass away with you.

Chapter 19
What Is True Wealth?

We make a living by what we get, but we make a life by what we give.
—Winston Churchill

What Do You Value Most in your Life?

The first answer that springs to mind likely isn't *"my car"* or *"my beautiful new home."* Usually, when we think about the things we truly value, we think about our families and friends, our health, our religious beliefs and values, our work ethic, or our skills. We might also add our accumulated wisdom, our life lessons we've learned throughout the years, our education in school, and our experiences in *"the school of hard knocks."*

Here's another question: What is the biggest investment you have ever made in your life?

Just as the things you value the most are not material possessions or financial assets, your biggest investment is not financial. Instead, it is made with the time, energy, love, and commitment you have poured into building your family.

Understanding this concept is the first step toward looking at family wealth in a way that envisions the big picture, instead of simply focusing on finances. Once you take a holistic approach to your family's wealth, you'll look at estate planning in an entirely new way.

The Four Categories of True Wealth

True wealth can be broken down into four basic categories:

1. Core Values: Our core values are the basis from which we operate. They encompass the foundation with which we were brought up, our family background, our talents, our health, and the attitudes with which we approach life and relate to those around us. This category of wealth might also include heirlooms that have significant meaning and emotional value within our family but have little or no financial value to anyone else.

2. **Life Experience:** Life experience includes the wisdom we've accumulated, along with our formal and informal education, the work ethic we've developed, and our commitment to spiritual beliefs or practices.

3. **Community:** The category of community encompasses the time, money, and energy we've spent contributing to society. It can include making financial gifts to charity, serving others through volunteer work, paying taxes to build roads, schools, and hospitals, protecting the environment, and providing for the common good of our neighbors.

4. **Financial Wealth:** Our financial wealth is the total of our financial assets or material possessions.

Financial Wealth Is Usually the Least Important Category

It is not a coincidence that Financial Wealth is listed last among the four basic categories. This is because, for the vast majority of people, financial assets pale in comparison with the other three types of wealth. If you had to choose, would you prefer to have Michael Jordan's basketball shoes or his jump shot? How about Shakespeare's pen or his wit?

What about Donald Trump? Given his financial position, it would be easy to think of his legacy to his children simply in terms of money. He is in a position to make sure that his children never have to face a day of work. Instead, he is known for passing his vision to them. Donald Trump's legacy to his children goes beyond his considerable wealth. He has endowed them with the more meaningful inheritances of his talent and his work ethic.

In your own life, would you trade your good health for money? How quick would you be to exchange your morals and reputation for material wealth? Most of us are much more eager for our children and grandchildren to inherit our core values and our wisdom—such as what it means to be generous or to be a responsible person—than we are for them to receive stocks, bonds, and real estate. Why? Because financial wealth can easily be acquired or regained with a wise application of skills, experience, and discipline. Values and wisdom, on the other hand, can't be purchased at any price.

This comprehensive view of wealth is what Legacy Wealth Planning is all about. Traditional estate planning, on the other hand, looks only at what material stuff you own and how to get it to your heirs. In other words, it focuses solely on leaving a financial inheritance.

In the next chapter, we'll look at two famous families who provide a startling illustration of the difference between leaving a financial inheritance and leaving a true legacy.

Chapter 20
The Vanderbilts and the Rothschilds: A Study in Contrasts

It requires a great deal of boldness and a great deal of caution to make a great fortune; and when you have got it, it requires ten times as much wit to keep it.

—Nathan Rothschild

You may have heard the expression *"shirtsleeves to shirtsleeves in three generations."* It refers to the all-too-common phenomenon whereby one family member earns substantial wealth by rolling up his sleeves and working hard, only to have his entire fortune dissipated by the time that wealth is handed down to the third generation.

Often, the reason for this loss of wealth is that heirs are not prepared to responsibly manage their inheritances, and there is no protection provided for the assets that are passed down. In short, traditional estate planning methods provide fertile ground for this maxim to come true.

As an illustration of this point, let's take a look at the contrasting stories of two of the most famous families of the Gilded Age, the Vanderbilts and the Rothschilds.

The Vanderbilts

In the 1800s there were very few people wealthier than Cornelius Vanderbilt, often known as *"the Commodore."* Vanderbilt, through hard work and brilliant financial maneuvering, built an empire in shipping and railroads. By the time he passed away in 1877, he had accumulated an estate valued at $105 million, the largest in American history at that time. Sadly, as time went by, that staggering wealth slipped away. According to a recent book about the family, when more than 100 Vanderbilt descendants met at a reunion in 1973, there was not a millionaire among them.

What happened to the unprecedented financial legacy left by Cornelius Vanderbilt? The estate was given outright to his children to manage in any way they wanted. With no measure of responsibility or accountability attached to his legacy, the Commodore's estate was squandered.

One of Vanderbilt's grandchildren said, *"It has left me with nothing to hope for, with nothing definite to seek or strive for. Inherited wealth is a real handicap to happiness."*

The Rothschilds

The Rothschild family, on the other hand, is a different story. Mayer Rothschild, the family patriarch, began a great European banking empire in the mid-eighteenth century that perpetuated the family fortune from generation to generation. Instead of earning a fortune and simply handing it off to the next generation, Mayer Rothschild taught his five children how to effectively manage money. The Rothschild family created the following system that lead to his family's great multi-generational success:

- Money was not given to heirs; the family either loaned the funds or entered into joint ventures with their relatives.

- Any loans that were made had strict provisions for repayment to the *"family bank."*

- At least once each year, family members gathered to discuss and reaffirm the family's values and plans. Anyone who failed to attend was locked out of the family bank.

How do the stories of these long-dead men of legendary status apply to us today? Whether we're Vanderbilts and Rothschilds or Smiths and

Joneses, the same estate planning lessons remain true. Outright transfer of financial assets is usually not enough. Instead, the goal is to engage in responsible wealth transfer so that our spouse, our children, and our grandchildren benefit from our hard work and the lessons we've learned over our lifetime.

A Family Wealth Trust is one effective method of accomplishing this goal, and in the coming chapters, we will see exactly how a Family Wealth Trust works to preserve your wealth, protect your loved ones, and create your legacy.

Chapter 21
Building Your Family's True Legacy

We all die. The goal isn't to live forever; the goal is to create something that will.

— **Chuck Palahniuk**

Legacy Wealth Planning is a process used by a small number of highly skilled attorneys around the country, and it is endorsed by the American Academy of Estate Planning Attorneys.

As we have seen, true wealth is a combination of financial assets and non-financial assets, which includes your family legacy. Legacy Wealth Planning differs from traditional estate planning because it takes a holistic view of wealth. It is designed to preserve every aspect of your family, including your family values and history, not only while you're alive, but for generations after your death.

The Two Elements of Legacy Wealth Planning

Legacy Wealth Planning is made up of two important elements. First, it addresses all of the financial assets you've worked to accumulate throughout your lifetime. It shields those assets from Guardianship and Conservatorship during your lifetime and from Probate at your death. After you've passed away, it shields those assets from unnecessary taxes and from the potential negative consequences of your spouse's potential remarriage, and it can even protect those assets in the event your spouse, a child, or a grandchild goes through a future divorce or has creditor issues. Legacy Wealth Planning also creates a way for you to distribute all of your personal possessions, like family photos, memorabilia, and miscellaneous family treasures, to the heirs you designate.

Second, and perhaps most important, Legacy Wealth Planning gives you the means to capture your family's history, biographies, life stories, wisdom, and values for future generations. This entire process creates responsible protection for your wealth, in all its forms, while you're alive and provides for an orderly transfer of that wealth after your death. With this planning you can prepare and educate your loved ones and even provide incentives for your heirs to improve themselves before family funds are available to them. This process truly creates a legacy within your family regardless of the size of your estate.

The Family Wealth Trust

The prime instrument for making all this happen and preserving both your financial and your non-financial wealth is a document called the Family Wealth Trust. The Family Wealth Trust is a flexible planning tool. At its core, it is designed to:

- Shield your estate and the estate of your spouse from Living Probate and Death Probate

- Minimize or even eliminate your estate tax bill

- Protect your estate from lawsuits and creditors

- Protect your estate in the event of your spouse's remarriage

- Allow you to take steps to capture your family's history, values, and non-financial wealth, preserving this precious part of your legacy for generations to come.

Depending on your concerns and the needs of your family, the Family Wealth Trust can also be used to:

- Shield your children's and grandchildren's inheritances from the threat of their own future divorces

- Protect your children and grandchildren from losing their inheritances to lawsuits, ex-spouses, creditors, or poor spending decisions

- Provide incentives for Beneficiaries to accomplish certain goals

- Provide for a disabled loved one without threatening that individual's government benefits

- Maximize the inheritance your retirement account provides to your Beneficiaries.

We'll spend the remainder of this book exploring in detail exactly how the Family Wealth Trust can be used to create a legacy within your family. The examples we'll use will be based on a *"traditional"* family, with married parents planning for their future, as well as the futures of their children or grandchildren.

If you are not married, or if you are not in a *"traditional"* family, don't worry. The Family Wealth Trust still applies to you, and there are some situations in which the protections it offers might be even more valuable to you than they would be to couples in a traditional marriage. Every step of the way, we'll point out the ways in which the Family Wealth Trust applies to single, divorced, and widowed individuals, as well as to those in nontraditional relationships.

Chapter 22
The Three Phases of Family Wealth Planning

Let our advance worrying become advance thinking and planning.
—Winston Churchill

Think of a Family Wealth Trust as an enhanced Living Trust. It is another, better, way to hold title to many of the assets you own. If the Family Wealth Trust owns title to your assets, rather than you personally holding title to them, then your death or disability has no impact on those assets. Plus, it can offer protections to your spouse, children, and grandchildren after you're gone. Your Family Wealth Trust typically spans three time periods: 1) Lifetime, 2) Death of the first spouse, and 3) Death of the second spouse. Let's take a look at how it performs during each of these three time periods:

Phase One: During Your Lifetime

While you are still alive, you and your spouse will work with your estate planning attorney to establish your Family Wealth Trust and to transfer your assets into the Trust. During this phase, you'll serve as Trustee and manage the Trust property.

Once your Trust is established, your attorney will prepare a deed transferring your residence, along with any other real estate you own, into your Family Wealth Trust. The deeds will then be recorded with the appropriate county office. Your stocks, bonds, mutual funds, CDs, and your other investment accounts will also be transferred from your name, as an individual, into the name of the Trust.

While you are alive and mentally competent, you'll control all of the property in the Trust as if you still owned it in your own name. You can make changes to the Trust, or even revoke it entirely, at any time. In other words, you are in complete control.

If you or your spouse later becomes ill, suffers a serious injury, or becomes mentally incapacitated, the healthy spouse can manage the property in the Trust, helping to avoid Living Probate.

Phase Two: After the Death of the First Spouse

When you or your spouse passes away, the Family Wealth Trust keeps the deceased spouse's property out of death Probate. Depending on the needs of the family, the Trust can be structured so that the estate of the first spouse to pass away is protected from creditors of the surviving spouse and from a potential remarriage.

What happens if the surviving spouse becomes disabled during this phase of the Family Wealth Trust? At this point, control of the Trust will be delegated to a Successor Trustee, already chosen by the spouses while both were alive and well, and Living Probate will again be avoided.

Phase Three: After the Death of the Second Spouse

When the time comes that both spouses have passed away, the Family Wealth Trust truly begins to show its value. Not only does the second spouse's property avoid Probate, but this is also the point at which estate tax planning measures that were initially included in the Trust come to fruition. This is the time during which Trusts for the protection of children or grandchildren often become active. Last, but certainly not least, at the death of the second spouse, the Family Wealth Trust functions to pass on all the components of the non-financial legacy you've worked hard to establish for your children and grandchildren.

What If You Are Not Married?

If you and your partner are not married, your Family Wealth Trust will be structured in a similar fashion; however, while the Family Wealth Trust can be used to reduce unmarried partners' estate taxes, the estate tax considerations will be somewhat different. This is because unmarried couples are not afforded an Unlimited Marital Deduction when the first partner passes away.

If you are single, divorced, or widowed, and you are not formulating your estate plan with a partner, then your Family Wealth Trust will involve two phases instead of three: 1) Lifetime and 2) Death of a single individual. In other words, the events you'll need to be concerned with are the ones that happen while you are alive and after you're gone.

In the coming chapters, we will see in detail exactly how the Family Wealth Trust works to achieve your estate planning goals through each of these three phases.

Chapter 23
Minding Your Own Business: Avoiding Living Probate with Your Family Wealth Trust

Always plan ahead. It wasn't raining when Noah built the ark.
—Richard C. Cushing

How does the Family Wealth Trust succeed in helping you avoid Living Probate when traditional estate planning so often fails in this area? Imagine you and your spouse have established a Family Wealth Trust. You're both alive and healthy, but what happens if you have a stroke or get into a serious accident? It's not a pleasant thought, but these things happen every day and we seldom expect them. You are now incapacitated and unable to sign your name to any documents, pay bills, or handle the family finances. How will your spouse manage things? Does this turn of events mean that your husband or wife, already distraught, will be forced to go to court to get permission to manage your family's assets?

Two Keys to Avoiding Living Probate

There are two key components of your Family Wealth Trust plan that should keep your spouse out of court and allow him or her to simply take control of the Trust and maintain financial control without the added burden of Living Probate.

First, the Family Wealth Trust plan includes Health Insurance Portability and Accountability Act (HIPAA) authorizations. This means that your husband or wife is able to get any necessary doctors' certifications to prove that you are indeed incapacitated, authorizing them to take over your affairs. Without these HIPAA authorizations—missing in many traditional estate plans—your spouse would be forced to go to court to get permission to act on your behalf.

Second, you will have worked closely with your attorney and followed their advice, meaning that your Trust is in the enviable position of being properly funded. This is important because it means that once your spouse gets the necessary doctor's certifications, he or she actually has Trust property over which to exercise authority. Remember, one of the major flaws of most barebones Living Trusts is that they are under-funded or simply not funded at all, leaving essential property outside of the Trustee's control when it matters most.

The Family Wealth Trust, on the other hand, is the prime instrument used in the process of Legacy Wealth Planning, and this process is utilized only by a core group of highly trained attorneys. Clients who have a Family Wealth Trust also have the advantage of a trusted advisor to help ensure that their Trust is properly funded and updated.

What If You're Not Married?

What happens in a situation where you are unmarried and you become incapacitated? Your Family Wealth Trust should be just as effective for you as it would be for a married person. You'll name a Successor Trustee to step in and take control of the Trust property in the case of your disability, your attorney will help to ensure that the proper HIPAA authorizations are in place, and you will work with him or her on making sure your Trust is properly funded and updated. Then, in the event of your incapacity, your Successor Trustee should be empowered to take control of your Trust property without the need for a Living Probate proceeding.

If you are in a non-traditional relationship of which your family does not approve, particularly if it is a same-sex relationship, this feature of your Family Wealth Trust can be especially important. It can help to prevent an unwanted and unpleasant court battle, and can assist in making sure that your partner, and not your biological family, remains in control of the financial decision-making in your household if that is what you desire.

Chapter 24
All in the Family: Avoiding Probate With a Family Wealth Trust

It's not what you gather in life, but what you scatter in life that tells the kind of life you've lived and the kind of person you are.
—Helen Walton, wife of Wal-Mart founder Sam Walton

We've seen how a Family Wealth Trust can help your family avoid the stresses and expenses that are involved in the Living Probate process. What happens, though, when you pass away? How does a Family Wealth Trust do a better job than traditional estate planning methods at keeping your assets out of the probate process and within the private realm of your family?

How a Family Wealth Trust Helps You Avoid Probate

We've already mentioned that the Family Wealth Trust is the cornerstone of the Legacy Wealth Planning process. This process is the key to keeping your assets out of Probate when you pass away.

Under the traditional estate planning model, even if you opt for a Basic Living Trust, in many instances your attorney will simply draw up the appropriate documents and ensure that they're properly signed. What happens after that is up to you.

A Basic Living Trust is useless for keeping property out of Probate if the Trust is not properly funded. Under the traditional estate planning model, this often means that if you are not diligent at transferring all the appropriate property into your Living Trust, then your Trust will not function as you intended. The same is true if you do not continue to transfer property into your Living Trust as you acquire it throughout your lifetime. Too often, after a Basic Living Trust is initially established, clients are left on their own to figure out which property should be transferred into it, and how these transfers should be accomplished. The result? A large number of Basic Living Trusts that do not function as intended because they are only partially funded or not funded at all.

Central to the Legacy Wealth Planning process is the relationship between you and your estate planning attorney. Your attorney needs to be skilled to educate and assist you when it comes to making sure that a Family Wealth Trust is properly funded. This means that the process of funding your Family Wealth Trust is not all on your shoulders. When your Trust is established, you'll title new assets, as appropriate, in the name of your Family Wealth Trust, instead of in your individual name. This way, there's no need to engage in an additional transfer of the new asset from yourself to your Trust.

Through the Legacy Wealth Planning process, the property that is meant to be in your Family Wealth Trust actually makes its way into your Trust. This means that when you pass away, your loved ones should not need to worry about the Probate process.

No Court Oversight Required

Instead, your Successor Trustee will step in and take charge of administering your Trust. With the help of an attorney, your Successor Trustee will be responsible for using your Trust assets to pay any applicable debts, necessary expenses, and taxes. He or she will then distribute your property to your spouse, children, or other Beneficiaries in accordance with the terms of your Trust.

The administration of your Trust does not require any court oversight. Since it is a private process, it has the potential to be much more efficient than the probate process, giving your Beneficiaries quicker access to your assets. Further, a Trust administration keeps your family's business away from prying eyes and produces less potential for estate litigation.

Chapter 25

I Do… Again: Guarding Your Estate When Your Spouse Remarries

I've had two proposals since I've been a widow. I am a wonderful catch, you know. I have a lot of money.

—Ruth Rendell

One of the real life issues that traditional estate planning is not very good at addressing is also one of those realities that many of us don't like to think about. What if, after you pass away, your spouse decides to remarry? Leaving the emotional implications aside for the moment, the financial consequences of this decision can be immense. How does Legacy Wealth Planning address this possibility? To answer this question, let's take a look at the Davis family.

Jim and Ellen Davis are happily married with two adult children. They've worked hard over the years and have built a solid nest egg, which they have been careful to protect. One step they have taken in guarding their family's financial security is establishing a Family Wealth Trust. Sadly, a few years after the Trust is established, Jim passes away.

Because Jim and Ellen worked closely with their attorney in establishing and funding their Trust, she does not need to deal with Probate during this difficult period in her life. Instead, her attorney helps her with the duties involved in administering the Trust and handling Jim's final affairs.

A little while after Jim's death, Ellen's neighbor Ralph drops by to offer his condolences. Ralph's wife passed away a year ago, and Ellen enjoys visiting with him. As the months go by, he continues to drop by, at first occasionally and then more frequently. Ellen and he have coffee in the morning, and sometimes he comes over for tea in the afternoon, or they go out to the movies in the evening.

Eventually, Ralph proposes marriage, and Ellen accepts. The only problem is that Ralph has two grown children of his own, and, while Ellen's children like Ralph, they're concerned that Ralph's children will find a way to get their hands on Jim's estate.

How the Family Wealth Trust Can Offer Remarriage Protection
Fortunately, Jim and Ellen's Family Wealth Trust was established with just this type of situation in mind, and it offers two types of protection.

The Trust was drafted so that when Jim passed away, his share of the estate was placed into a separate Sub-Trust. This Sub-Trust is irrevocable, and the Beneficiaries are Jim and Ellen's two children. Ellen serves as Trustee of the Sub-Trust, and she gets to use and benefit from the property in the Sub-Trust, but she does not own the property, nor does she own the Sub-Trust. The property in the Sub-Trust is not Ellen's, so it is beyond the reach of Ralph and his children. Instead, it is ultimately reserved for Ellen and Jim's children.

The Trust also contains a special condition. It says that if Ellen remarries without signing a prenuptial agreement, she'll lose the ability to access the property in the Sub-Trust. This condition further protects Ellen from the threat of being taken advantage of in her new relationship, and it does so in a very clever way. Instead of making Ellen the *"bad guy,"* the special condition gives her an excuse that's both legitimate and convenient for bringing up the topic of a prenuptial agreement and insisting that she is financially protected in her new relationship.

Chapter 26
Lawsuits: Protecting Your Spouse After You're Gone

I was never ruined but twice—once when I lost a lawsuit, once when I won one.

—Voltaire

As we have already seen, anyone can become the defendant in a lawsuit. All it takes is a moment's distraction, and you can find yourself on the losing end of a legal action worth hundreds of thousands, or even millions, of dollars. What's worse, you can find yourself subject to a large judgment due to a completely frivolous lawsuit, and the more money you have, the larger a target you tend to be for lawsuits of all types.

Imagine your spouse being faced with just such a court action mere months after you've passed away. If you have a traditional estate plan, it likely does not offer protection from creditors or lawsuits. The result? Not only does your spouse face the strain and anxiety that accompany any court proceeding, he or she must also deal with the possibility of losing the financial security you spent a lifetime building for your family.

Lawsuit and Creditor Protection
A Family Wealth Trust, on the other hand, can function to encapsulate your portion of your family's assets in a Sub-Trust when you pass away. This Sub-Trust is irrevocable, but it can be managed by your spouse, and your spouse can enjoy the benefits of the assets in the Sub-Trust during his or her lifetime. Because the property in the Sub-Trust is not owned or controlled by your spouse, it is protected from his or her creditors, and it is shielded from lawsuits.

Chapter 27
Paving the Way for Reduced Estate Taxes

The only difference between death and taxes is that death doesn't get worse every time Congress meets.

—**Will Rogers**

Who is the largest potential creditor of your estate? If you guessed the government, you're correct! One of the trickiest and most vexing aspects of estate planning is the fact that the law, and estate tax law in particular, is always subject to change. Congress seems bent on keeping us on our toes, and an excellent illustration of this fact are the recent changes in the federal estate tax law.

A Brief Modern History of the Federal Estate Tax

You might remember the tension and discussion surrounding the estate tax that began in 2009 and continued right through the end of the following year. What was all the fuss about? The story starts back in 2001, in the early days of George W. Bush's presidency. During this time, Congress passed the Economic Growth and Tax Relief Reconciliation Act of 2001, which became known as *"EGTRRA."* One of the things this law did was to revamp the federal estate tax rules. It provided for gradual increases in the federal estate tax exemption to a peak of $3.5 million in 2009, and then it eliminated the tax altogether for the year 2010. However, that's where that law stopped. After 2010, EGTRRA provided that the estate tax exemption would permanently fall back to $1 million.

The years went by and 2009 came and went. Congress shocked many of us by actually allowing the estate tax to disappear at the beginning of 2010. There was much speculation during 2010 as to whether the estate tax would return to the $1 million level. Then, on December 17, 2010, the Tax Relief, Unemployment Insurance Reauthorization and Job

Creation Act of 2010 (also known as the Tax Relief Act of 2010) was signed into law. The law set the estate tax exemption at $5 million per person and introduced the feature of *"spousal portability"* of the estate tax exemption. This law only applied through the end of 2012, leaving Congress to re-calibrate the estate tax for 2013 and beyond. On January 2, 2013, the American Taxpayer Relief Act of 2012 (ATRA 2012) was signed into law which set the maximum estate tax rate at 40% with a $5 million dollar exemption adjusted annually using an inflation index. Under this law, the spousal portability feature was made permanent.

Under the spousal portability provision of the American Taxpayer Relief Act of 2012 (ATRA 2012), when the first spouse passed away, his or her unused estate tax exemption could pass to the surviving spouse. (There must have been a timely-filed estate tax return electing portability of the exemption.) This portability exemption could be added to the estate tax exemption of the surviving spouse so that, as a practical matter, the second spouse to die got to apply both spouses' estate tax exemptions to his or her estate.

Estate Tax Laws Demand Flexibility

The actions of Congress since 2001 provide a clear illustration of the *"here today, gone tomorrow"* nature of estate tax legislation, making a flexible tax plan essential for affluent and wealthy couples. Although the most recent law states the changes it makes are *"permanent,"* who knows how long that will be the case.

An advantage of the Legacy Wealth Planning process is that it incorporates a proactive and flexible approach to estate tax planning, allowing you to maximize the inheritances you leave to your loved ones and ensuring that the IRS does not get more than its share of your estate.

The Legacy Wealth Planning process offers flexible planning tools to suit a variety of circumstances. Legacy Wealth Planning attorneys are trained to identify the unique needs of their clients and tailor a plan to meet those needs. For example, for clients who are very likely to be faced with a federal estate tax bill, or for those who are subject to estate taxes on the state level, there is the AB Trust.

Tax Planning With an AB Trust

For married couples whose estates are large enough to warrant estate tax planning concerns, a Family Wealth Trust will be established so that, upon the death of the first spouse, the Trust is divided up into two Sub-Trusts. These Trusts are often called the *"A Trust"* and the *"B Trust."*

Under this scenario, the surviving spouse's property is held in the A Trust and the deceased spouse's property, up to the amount of the applicable estate tax exemption, is held in the B Trust.

The Bennett Family Wealth Trust
How does a typical Family Wealth Trust deal with the issue of tax planning? Consider the circumstances of Kevin and Sarah Bennett. When you add up all of their assets, including the value of their home, all of their investments, and their life insurance, Kevin and Sarah have a net worth of $1.7 million.

In the state of Minnesota where they live, there is a state-level estate tax with an exemption amount that is currently increasing gradually to $2 million by 2018. Therefore, their Family Wealth Trust includes A-B Trust provisions.

Several years after establishing their Family Wealth Trust, Kevin passes away in 2019. Because they worked closely with their attorney to ensure that the Trust was properly funded, Sarah does not need to deal with the Probate process during this difficult time in her life. Also, because of the Unlimited Marital Deduction, any property in Kevin's estate passes to Sarah free of estate tax at the time of Kevin's death. There is one more step, though.

In her capacity as Successor Trustee, Sarah meets with her estate planning attorney, who divides the Trust into two Sub-Trusts. The A Trust belongs to Sarah. It is revocable and is funded with Sarah's portion of the couple's property, which equals $850,000. Sarah acts as Trustee and exercises full control over the A Trust and the property it contains.

The B Trust, on the other hand, is an irrevocable Trust. Kevin's property, up to the amount of the applicable estate tax exclusion, is transferred into this Trust. In this situation, $850,000, or Kevin's half of the couple's property, goes into the B Trust. Sarah acts as Trustee over this Trust as well, but her right to control the Trust and the Trust assets is limited. Sarah may use and benefit from the property held by the B Trust, but that property is not hers and she cannot change the terms of the Trust.

What happens when Sarah passes away a few years later?

This is the time period where the A and the B Trusts come together, and Kevin and Sarah's estate makes its way into the hands of their children, Katherine and David. At the time of Sarah's death, the estate has grown to $2.4 million. Katherine is named as Successor Trustee. She reads the Trust document for guidance as to how to divide the Trust property. (We'll talk more about this in coming chapters.)

However, nine months after Sarah passes away, Katherine is contacted by an agent from the state revenue department. Surprise! The state wants its share of Sarah's estate in the form of an estate tax payment. After all, when Sarah passed away, the total estate was worth more than $2 million, right?

Katherine explains to the tax agent that there are no taxes due. She says that when Sarah passed away, the value of assets in the A Trust was equal to $1.2 million. Because Sarah gets a $2 million exclusion from the state estate tax, there are no taxes due.

Ever vigilant, the tax agent wants to know about the assets in the B Trust. Katherine explains that the B Trust was not owned by Sarah. The B Trust was set up when her father passed away. When he died, $850,000 was put into that Trust. At that time, Kevin's exemption was large enough that it shielded his part of the estate from taxes. But the tax agent astutely points out that those assets have now increased in value from $850,000 to $1.2 million, surely there must be tax due on the increase. Katherine patiently explains that the assets in the B Trust are never subject to estate tax regardless of how large they may grow because Sarah was never the owner of those assets for tax purposes. She was only the Trustee of the B Trust and the Beneficiary with certain limited rights. Consequently, those assets will never be considered a part of her estate. On top of all of the other benefits of the Family Wealth Trust, it protected Kevin and Sarah's entire $2.4 million estate from their state's estate tax.

Tax Planning With a Flex Trust

What if there is a question as to whether or not the value of your estate will warrant AB Planning for tax purposes when the time comes?

Under certain limited circumstances, your Family Wealth Trust might be established to include Flex Trust provisions instead of AB Trust Provisions. Under this arrangement, when the Trust is created, you and your spouse select a trusted person or Special Co-Trustee. This is an independent third party other than the surviving spouse or one of your Beneficiaries. When the first spouse passes away, this Special Co-Trustee decides how much money, if any, to fund into the B Trust. His or her decision is based on the circumstances at the time, including the value of your estate and the status of the law.

Flexibility is key when it comes to anticipating and minimizing your estate tax bill. As we are about to see, though, the true value of Trust planning extends far beyond the realm of estate taxes.

Chapter 28
The Family Access Trust: Inheritance Protection in the Face of Divorce

Marriage is grand. Divorce is about twenty grand.

—Jay Leno

What is your number one worry when it comes to the preservation of your family's wealth after you're gone? If you're like many American parents, you worry most about your children's or grandchildren's inheritances falling prey to one of three risks:

- Divorce

- Opportunists

- Lawsuits

In fact, when Financial Planning Magazine asked clients about the security of their wealth, their first concern was that someone would take financial advantage of their children or grandchildren.

As we have seen, this is a legitimate concern, yet traditional estate planning methods often leave the inheritances of children and grandchildren wide open to exposure in divorce settlements, to exploitation by financial predators, to the claims of creditors, and to the inexperience and poor judgment of heirs themselves.

Divorce: A Very Real Threat

Let's focus for a moment on the risk of divorce and how Legacy Wealth Planning can protect the inheritances of your children from being swept up and carried off by a son-in-law or daughter-in-law as part of a divorce settlement.

We've all seen the statistics. America has the highest divorce rate in the world, and, although each of us hopes that our children will be the ones to beat the odds, it is simply not wise to stake the financial futures of our loved ones on hope. This is one area where our children and grandchildren are, indeed, better safe than sorry.

What can you do to protect the inheritances of your children and grandchildren? The best thing you can do is to avoid the trap of leaving an inheritance to your heirs outright after you're gone. Under this approach, the moment the assets come into an heir's possession, there is nothing you can do to protect those assets.

The alternative is to hold the assets for the benefit of your heir without handing ownership of the assets over to him or her. The way to do this is to keep each child's or grandchild's share of your estate in Trust after you have passed away, permitting that heir to have access to the property but not to own it.

Don't Squeeze the Toothpaste

One way to think about this is to picture a Trust as a tube of toothpaste. The assets are the toothpaste, and the Trust is the tube, protecting the toothpaste and keeping it all together. What happens when you squeeze some of the toothpaste out of the tube? It is no longer protected, and there's no way to get it back into the tube. Making outright distributions of assets to your heirs is like squeezing all of the toothpaste out of the tube. Once the transfer is made, the property is exposed to all manner of threats and, what's worse, the damage is done. There is nothing more you can do to protect the inheritance.

Transferring your property in Trust to your child or grandchild keeps the toothpaste in the tube and gives the tube to your heir. He or she still gets to enjoy the property, but with the added protection afforded by the Trust.

Beth's Story: The Family Access Trust

How does this approach protect a child's inheritance in the unfortunate event of a divorce? Let's look at Beth's story.

Beth was her parents' golden child. She was the one who got excellent grades, has a great career, has managed her finances well, and has been blessed with a beautiful family. However, no one's life is perfect, and Beth is not an exception. She and her husband, Mark, have had a difficult marriage. Beth's parents did not approve of some of Mark's behavior, and they watched with dismay as he and Beth separated and reconciled several times. Knowing that a divorce was likely looming, Beth's parents decided to build divorce protection for her into their estate plan. They spoke to their estate planning attorney, who included a special set of instructions in their Family Wealth Trust. This special set of instructions is called the Family Access Trust, and, under its terms, here is what happens to Beth's inheritance when her parents pass away:

- Beth's share of the estate is not distributed to her outright; instead, it is funded into a Family Access Trust, with Beth named as the Beneficiary.

- The Family Access Trust is an irrevocable Trust. The terms of the Trust cannot be changed, nor can the Trust be terminated.

- The terms of the Trust allow Beth access to all of the Trust income for her lifetime. She can also access the principal of the Trust.

- Beth is named Trustee of the Trust.

- Beth must follow the terms of the Trust, and she is not the owner of the Trust property.

- When Beth passes away, the property left in the Trust will go to her two children.

It turns out that Beth's parents saw the writing on the wall. Not long after her mom passes away, Mark and Beth file for divorce. Because Beth's inheritance is held in the Family Access Trust, and is not owned by Beth, in her state it is not available for the court to even consider dividing among the couple. Instead, Beth's inheritance remains intact.

Contrast this with what commonly happens when a child receives an inheritance outright from his or her parents. It would have been easy for Beth to receive a large sum of money from her parents and unthinkingly place it into joint accounts, or use some of it towards the purchase of a vehicle or other assets titled jointly with Mark. These actions, quite normal in the context of married life, could have had unintended and far-reaching consequences. Down the road, they could have made her inheritance fair game to property division by the divorce court, and Mark could have walked away with up to half of the hard-earned wealth Beth's parents passed down to their daughter.

Thanks to her parents' forethought and responsible planning, however, Beth's inheritance was preserved so that her children can reap the benefits of her family's hard work and legacy.

Chapter 29

The Family Sentry Trust: Protecting Your Heirs from Creditors, Predators, and Themselves

Creditors have better memories than debtors.

—Benjamin Franklin

Divorce is not the only threat to an heir's inheritance. There are other big worries that keep parents up at night, such as the possibility that someone will target their children for get rich quick schemes or foolish financial investments, or that their children will be subject to a frivolous lawsuit. Perhaps the most tragic way for a child to lose his or her investment is to squander it due to lack of experience, poor financial decision making, or deeper personal problems.

How do you protect a child from creditors, predators, and perhaps most significantly, himself or herself? This brings us to Steve, the black sheep of his family. Steve has always been a nonconformist. He's had two marriages, neither of which ended well. He has a young son with special needs whom his parents are particularly concerned about, and Steve has only recently begun to maintain steady employment.

When Steve's parents established their Family Wealth Trust, their concerns about Steve were threefold.

- First, they were aware that Steve was much more comfortable spending money than he was saving it. Since he had not had a steady job for much of his adult life, he was no stranger to debt or to debt collectors. His parents wanted to prevent Steve from spending his entire inheritance and leaving his young son with no share in the family legacy.

- Second, they wanted to protect Steve's inheritance not only from his spending, but also from being drained by any creditor lawsuits that might be filed against him. They were eager to allow Steve himself to take responsibility for his own spending decisions, but they did not want his decisions to jeopardize their hard-earned wealth or their family legacy.

- Third, since they intended to leave Steve a sizable inheritance, they wanted to ensure that he would not receive the money, quit his job, and live on the inherited funds.

When they expressed these concerns to their estate planning attorney and asked whether a solution could be crafted that addressed all three concerns, the attorney's response was to build provisions known as a Family Sentry Trust into their Family Wealth Trust.

Protecting Steve From Himself: The Family Sentry Trust

A Family Sentry Trust is an irrevocable, lifetime Trust that can protect your children's or grandchildren's inheritances from lawsuits, get-rich-quick schemes, or poor financial decisions and provide incentives to encourage certain positive behaviors. Here is how the Family Sentry Trust works for the Jones family:

The Family Sentry Trust established for Steve is a little different than the Family Access Trust a parent would establish to protect a child's inheritance from the threat of divorce. One of the most noticeable differences is that Steve is not the Trustee of his own Trust. Instead, a third-party Trustee has the power to decide whether or not to distribute assets to Steve. These provisions are called a fully discretionary Trust, and it protects Steve from himself while protecting his inheritance from his creditors, provides for Steve's legitimate needs, and preserves his parents' legacy for Steve's children. If, next year, Steve approaches the Trustee and just has to have a brand-new luxury car, even though it is obviously not in his best interest, the Trustee has the ability to say *"no."*

What about the possibility of Steve quitting his job? The Family Sentry Trust includes a clever and very positive provision designed to help Steve maximize his potential. Under the terms of the Trust, Steve is required to present his W-2 to the Trustee each year. The Trustee then distributes to Steve an amount equal to his annual earnings for that year. If Steve earns $40,000 in a given year, he'll get $40,000 in Trust funds. If his earnings are $10,000, the Trust will pay him $10,000. If he earns nothing on his job, then he gets no income from the Trust.

The Family Sentry Trust can also be used to encourage heirs to pursue higher education, providing that if a child attends school full-time and maintains a certain minimum grade point average, she'll receive an income from the Trust. Graduation often means a bonus distribution. What if your child or grandchild struggles with alcoholism or drug addiction? Often, clients require treatment and ongoing drug testing as a condition for the distribution of Trust funds. In fact, the Family Sentry Trust can be adapted to provide incentives for your heirs to achieve an almost limitless number and variety of goals, provided those goals are not illegal or in violation of public policy.

Chapter 30
A Special Plan for a Special Child

You've developed the strength of a draft horse while holding on to the delicacy of a daffodil... you are the mother, advocate, and protector of a child with a disability.

—Lori Bergman

Parents of a disabled child can find themselves between a rock and a hard place when it comes to estate planning. You want to provide a legacy for your child, but the last thing you want to do is to leave him or her an outright inheritance. Why?

An Inheritance Can Jeopardize Benefits

Government benefits programs like Medicaid and SSI have very stringent rules concerning the amount of assets a recipient is allowed to have while remaining eligible for benefits. If a disabled Beneficiary receives even a modest inheritance, it can push the Beneficiary over the asset limit imposed by the government. Once this happens, the benefits are cut off until the inheritance is used up. Once the inheritance is gone, the benefits are reinstated.

Think about the impact this can have on your disabled child. Typically, while government benefits cover the basics when it comes to the care of your child, you as a parent provide countless *"extras"* for him or her on a regular basis. For instance, you might make sure to buy your child his or her favorite toiletries, make sure he or she has access to favorite books, games, and movies, go on family trips together, and make sure your child's education is enriched and supplemented.

If you were to pass away leaving an outright inheritance to your child, not only would government benefits stop, so would all those *"extras"* you work so hard to provide. Once the inheritance was used up and the government benefits resumed, your child would no longer have you to provide those special comforts. Instead, he or she would have only the basic services covered by government funds—a bleak picture, indeed.

With careful planning, though, there is a way to make sure your child keeps those essential government benefits while continuing to have the *"extras"* you provided during your lifetime. This can be accomplished by leaving your child's inheritance in a Family Special Needs Trust.

How the Family Special Needs Trust Works

The Family Special Needs Trust allows you to provide funds for a disabled child or grandchild while ensuring that his or her government benefits are not interrupted. In establishing the Trust, you'll appoint Trustees for the child's Trust. Generally, during your lifetime, you'll serve as Trustee, managing the assets placed in the Trust for your child's benefit. You'll also name a Successor Trustee, an individual you know and trust, who will take over the management of the Trust in case of your disability or death.

The Successor Trustee will be in charge of taking care of the Trust assets and overseeing your child's finances according to detailed written instructions you provide when you establish the Trust. Included in those instructions are limitations on the purposes for which Trust assets can be used. The terms of the Trust will specify that funds can only be withdrawn and spent for purposes other than those covered under federal, state, or charitable benefits programs.

In this way, a Family Special Needs Trust ensures that your child will receive the benefits he or she relies on, while continuing to lead a full and enriched life, even if you can't be there.

Chapter 31
Keeping the Farm in the Family

"There are risks and costs of any program of action. But they are far less than the long range risks and costs of comfortable inaction."
—John F. Kennedy

A Tale of a Farming Family

Dean and Rita are Red River Valley farmers who know the value of hard work. Their hard work has paid off to the tune of $2.5 million in land and $500,000 in machinery and other assets for a total of a $3 million net worth. They also have a family that includes four children: Molly, Jean, Jim, and Lloyd.

Molly and her husband, Ron, have helped Dean and Rita farm for the past twelve years and have added value to the farming operation. In fact, Molly is the only one of Dean and Rita's children that has shown any interest in farming. Molly and her husband have accumulated some farm assets themselves; however, most of their livelihood is made by farming with Dean and Rita. Dean and Rita would like the farm to eventually pass on to Molly and her husband, Ron; however, there is a concern about being fair to the non-farming children. Given the high value of land in the area, Dean and Rita are also concerned about Molly's ability to buy out her brothers' and sister's interest and about keeping the family farm going. They want to provide a fair system whereby Molly and her husband, Ron, can farm the land and eventually purchase it and keep the farm in the family.

Jean and Jim have never shown much interest in the farm or all the work that goes into keeping it running properly. Jim has always been a *"city boy*" at heart and has always been quick to remind Dean and Rita of that fact. As soon as he turned 18, he left for college in the big city and never looked back. He is a successful business owner and is doing well financially due to his shrewd financial decision-making. Jim has never gotten along with Molly's husband and Dean and Rita are concerned about the effect this conflict may have on the farming operation should Molly have to purchase or rent Jim's share of the land.

Jean followed a similar path as Jim in regard to obtaining a college degree and moving to the big city; however, the similarities stop abruptly with the state of her finances. Jean and her husband are quick to spend and slow to save. Their desire to not only keep up with the Joneses but to sprint right on by them has resulted in some past issues with creditors. Dean and Rita have been there to bail them out in the past, but they are concerned about what might happen to Jean's share of the farm when they are no longer around.

Lloyd lives just down the road from Dean and Rita, and he occasionally does some work around the farm. He has been a problem child since his youth and this behavior carried over into his adult years as well. He has been married once and is presently separated, but not divorced, from his current spouse. Lloyd has suffered from alcoholism from a young age and spends the majority of his money on this habit. Dean and Rita have always been there to offer their support both emotionally and financially, but they worry Lloyd's share will be destroyed by the consequences of a future divorce and his present lifestyle.

Making Hay While the Sun Is Still Shining

Based on their life situation, Dean and Rita have the following goals for the farm transition portion of their estate plan:

- Be fair and equitable to Molly and their non-farming children, while keeping in mind that fair is not always equal

- Keep the farm in the family and make the transition affordable for Molly and Ron

- Minimize or eliminate family disputes, court hassles, legal fees, and taxes

Buying the Farm

Dean and Rita have options.

They could just leave everything equally to their four children, however this would likely destroy the farm Dean and Rita have worked and sacrificed to grow. What if Molly and Ron are unable to afford or negotiate a reasonable sale or land rent amount with the other children? Can they afford to have their sole source of income vanish once Dean and Rita are gone? What if Jim's hard feelings toward Ron result in a premium price that Molly cannot afford and Jim demands the land be sold so he can cash out his share? What if Jean demands the land be sold to pay off debt or a creditor attaches her interest and forces a sale? What if Lloyd needs the money to get by or unfortunately to feed his habit and demands the land be sold to cash out his share? Sadly, what if a portion of Lloyd's share is potentially taken should his separation turn into a divorce? What can Dean and Rita do?

Life insurance is one option, and it can be a significant tool if used appropriately. Life insurance can be used to provide the funds for Molly to buy out her siblings or to compensate the non-farming children; the farming assets then go to the farming child and the life insurance proceeds go to the non-farming children. In using this strategy, it is important to properly plan to minimize or eliminate estate tax consequences.

If life insurance is not a feasible option due to one not being insurable or the insurance being too expensive due to age or health, then a properly structured enhanced plan may be appropriate for a successful farm transition. One option under an enhanced plan would be to place the farm in a separate Trust with the governing rules set by Dean and Rita under the guidance of a qualified estate planning attorney to ensure a smooth transition of the farming operation. One such rule could set a fair selling price for each child's share of the farmland for Molly to pay. The *"sweat equity"* that is commonly referred to when hard-working children assist in the development of the farm's value needs to be objectively valued and rewarded to have true fairness. There are many ways to determine what a fair selling price might be, such as a discounted amount off of the market appraised value, setting a specific price in advance, or giving a larger share to the farming child that leaves them with less to purchase. Financing can also be arranged with a properly structured estate plan and can take the form of allowing the farming child to lease the farm property for a period of time and later sign a contract for deed arrangement. This provides flexibility for the farming child to purchase the property with rent and purchase payments going to the non-farming children. Other stipulations can also be added to this farm transition plan, such as how to address other heirs, such as grandchildren, who may wish to farm in the event of an early death or retirement of the farming child. Another option is to offer a right of first refusal to other family members should the farming child decide to sell the farm in the future. These issues can be decided now while Dean and Rita are still around, rather than forcing their heirs to figure it out after they are both gone.

Planting the Seed

Unfortunately, most farming families fail to discuss these potential real life issues when it comes to farm business ownership succession. All too often, they pretend either that these issues do not exist or that they will never happen to them. While these issues can be difficult to discuss, they become much more difficult to live through if discussions never take place and proper planning is not done. As you can see, it is important to have a plan of ownership succession in place for the next generation of family farmers.

Parents must have a vision of what they wish to have happen to the family farm and discuss these ideas with their children before it is too late. Do the children desiring to farm or who are farming have the same vision as the parents? Have any discussions taken place in regard to passing on the farm, or has this always been a topic that is not considered polite conversation? Have you taken any steps to create unity within your family and with your team of advisors? Have you given any thought to the emotions within your own family and your current plan's impact on present and future family relationships such as those between you and your children, between your children themselves, and between your children and grandchildren. Only through comprehensive planning, sharing of values, sharing of time, and vision will the family stay together and preserve unity to move ownership succession of the family farm and transfer of management to the next generation.

Changing Seasons

What if things change? …And they will! Proper planning and review of your plan at set intervals can accommodate law changes, family changes, career changes, and provide for new legal strategies. Like Dean and Rita, you are encouraged to seek legal counsel who has a passion for helping families, provides comprehensive estate planning services, assists you with proper maintenance of your plan, and desires to have an ongoing relationship with your family.

Chapter 32
Stretching Your Retirement Assets

If you would be wealthy, think of saving as well as getting.
—Benjamin Franklin

If you have a Qualified Retirement Plan, such as a traditional 401(k) or IRA, you know that these plans are tax-deferred. This means the money you contribute to the Plan is not taxed when it goes into your account. Instead, that money is allowed to grow with no tax consequences until you withdraw it. The IRS does not benefit from letting your money grow tax-free indefinitely, so it has imposed certain rules governing when you must take distributions from your Retirement Plan.

Required Minimum Distributions

You, as the account holder, must start taking annual distributions beginning after you reach age 70 ½. These distributions are called Required Minimum Distributions (RMD's), and they are calculated based on the amount of funds in your Retirement Plan as well as your remaining life expectancy.

In addition to using your retirement funds for your own lifetime expenses, you also have the chance to designate a Beneficiary to inherit the account when you pass away. If you leave the account to your Beneficiary as an outright distribution, he or she will have a Required Minimum Distribution each year. The amount of the RMD will be based on your Beneficiary's remaining life expectancy. Your Beneficiary will also have the option to withdraw more than his or her RMD, which can have unwanted consequences.

The Dangers of Withdrawing Too Much

When your Beneficiary withdraws money from an inherited account, he or she is responsible for income tax on the distribution. Taking out a large lump sum can result in a burdensome tax bill for your loved one.

Only money that remains in the account has the chance to grow, tax-deferred, thus maximizing your Beneficiary's inheritance. When unnecessary funds are withdrawn, the growth potential of the account is diminished, and your Beneficiary's inheritance shrinks.

Stretching Out Your Beneficiary's Inheritance

How can you ensure that the retirement funds you pass on to your Beneficiary are protected and provide a maximum inheritance with minimal tax bills? You can establish a Family Retirement Preservation Trust. This is a specially qualified Trust that is named as the Beneficiary of your IRA. You'll appoint a Trustee to manage your retirement account after you pass away, and the Trustee will be instructed to withdraw only the Required Minimum Distributions on behalf of the Trust Beneficiary each year, thus stretching out your Beneficiary's inheritance.

The Family Retirement Preservation Trust guarantees that the payout of your retirement account is deferred as long as possible, and keeps the bulk of your retirement account in trust, where it is sheltered and protected. This provides your Beneficiary three valuable advantages:

1. It lets the assets in your retirement account continue to grow for as long as the IRS allows. This helps to ensure that your Beneficiary receives the largest inheritance possible by way of your retirement account.

2. It minimizes your Beneficiary's income tax bills.

3. It provides your Beneficiary with an annual income while guaranteeing that your hard-earned retirement funds are

protected from creditors, scams, or your Beneficiary's own poor decision-making.

This arrangement gives your Beneficiary the best of both worlds, allowing him or her to enjoy the largest inheritance possible while paying the least possible amount of income tax.

Chapter 33
Paying for Long-Term Health Care: The Medicaid Trust

Knowledge is the antidote to fear

—**Ralph Waldo Emerson**

What are your most pressing fears? If the thought of entering a nursing home makes your stomach churn, you are not alone. According to the study Aging in Place in America, people over the age of 65 are more afraid of moving into a nursing home than are afraid of death.

One of the most daunting aspects of nursing home care is that it is so expensive. Nationwide, the median cost of a private room in a nursing home is more than $220 per day. That translates to more than $80,000 for a year of care. It is easy to read numbers like these and become paralyzed with worry. Unless you are in the middle of a health crisis, it is tempting to ignore the subject of nursing home care and just hope you'll never need it.

Estate planning, however, should include long-term care planning if you're concerned about paying for nursing home care. A well-drafted estate plan can allow you to protect all or a portion of your children's inheritance, not only from divorce and remarriage, but from the possibility of you or your spouse needing long-term health care. More importantly, when it comes to long-term health care planning, ignoring your fears can be a costly mistake.

Planning ahead gives you control. It lets you shape what your nursing home experience might look like, and it allows you to think carefully and methodically about how you'll pay for care. More accurately, it gives you time to explore your options for obtaining nursing home coverage, so you can preserve your hard-earned assets. One of the most common ways to pay for nursing home care is to qualify for Medicaid.

Medicaid

Most people can't afford to pay out of pocket for nursing home care—at least, not for long. Often, this is where Medicaid comes in. Medicaid is one of the most-used alternatives for defraying, or even eliminating, the cost of nursing home care. It is also one of the most misunderstood.

What Is Medicaid?

Medicaid is a joint federal and state program that pays certain healthcare costs. It is available to those who meet certain financial criteria, including income and asset limits. The federal government sets the overall Medicaid guidelines, and then coordinates with each state to fund the program. Each state has the authority to interpret and enforce the Medicaid eligibility guidelines, within reason. Therefore, the actual rules for qualifying for Medicaid can and actually do differ from state to state.

Who Needs Medicaid?

Medicaid offers more comprehensive long-term care coverage than the Medicare program, which is geared toward paying for routine medical care and short-term hospital stays. This, coupled with the high cost of long-term care, has made Medicaid the main source for funding nursing home care for middle class seniors.

Medicaid Qualification Rules

The Medicaid qualification rules are complicated; however, here is a brief overview of the main rules to keep in mind:

- **Income Limits**—In many states, Medicaid applies income limits to nursing home residents and their spouses.

- **Asset Limits**—An appraisal of your assets is performed and they are categorized into countable and exempt assets. Exempt assets are not factored into your qualification. Countable assets, however, are totaled and the value must not exceed the asset limits currently in place.

- **Gifting and the Look-Back Period**—Although gifting can be a useful strategy for reducing your countable assets, it has to be done with careful consideration and advice from an attorney. Why? In order to keep people from just giving away their assets to qualify for Medicaid, there is a look-back period. Any assets you've given away within 5 years of your application trigger a penalty period, which is a delay in benefits, based on the value of the assets that were gifted.

- **Estate Recovery**—After a Medicaid recipient and their spouse, if they were married, have passed away, the state is required to recover what it paid for that individual's care from their estate. A family's most valuable asset is typically their home, not just financially, but also emotionally, and it is the asset most often *"recovered"* against. In other words, it is the home's value which is often used to repay the state. There are some exceptions to this rule, but they are not applicable to most families.

The rules certainly sound complicated, so many people mistakenly think that you must completely impoverish yourself and your family before you can qualify for Medicaid long-term care coverage. This is not true. In reality, Medicaid guidelines allow you to keep certain property and allow your spouse, who does not need nursing home coverage, to retain at least part of his or her income.

There are also *"safe harbor"* provisions built into the Medicaid guidelines that allow you to plan ahead and protect at least a portion of your assets, while remaining eligible for long-term care coverage. As mentioned earlier, planning ahead is critical and a cornerstone of this proactive planning is a Medicaid Trust.

The Medicaid Trust

The goal of Medicaid planning is to work within the guidelines and outside of the 5-year look-back period to convert enough of your countable assets into exempt assets. This way, you can qualify for Medicaid without a penalty and avoid recovery, if the time comes for you to need nursing home care.

One of the most effective strategies is a Medicaid Trust, which can be included as part of your Legacy Wealth Plan. This Trust may be in addition to your Family Wealth Trust.

A Medicaid Trust must follow some strict guidelines, for example, the Trust must be *"irrevocable"* and you will only have access to the Trust's income, and not the principal. However, when you transfer assets into the Trust, it is no longer considered to be part of your estate for Medicaid purposes.

Keep in mind, though, that assets transferred into a Medicaid Trust are also subject to the look-back rule, so planning ahead with a Medicaid Trust is critical.

The benefits of the Medicaid Trust are that it:

- Reduces your countable assets, allowing you to qualify for Medicaid benefits when the time comes;

- Avoids spending thousands of dollars per month on nursing home care;

- Protects your family home and other assets from Medicaid recovery after your death;

- Allows you to ensure your assets are protected and preserved for your chosen beneficiaries; and

- Allows you and your spouse to use the Trust income to supplement your living expenses, if necessary.

No matter where you are in the planning process, remember that Medicaid planning is a complex topic. The rules are complicated, they change frequently, and they vary from state to state. Strategies that work for one family might not work for another. The guidance of your experienced estate planning attorney is critical in navigating the rules and determining what options are best for you and your family.

Chapter 34

Wealth Beyond Numbers: The Legacy Wealth Planning Portfolio

When we are planning for posterity, we ought to remember that virtue is not hereditary.

—Thomas Paine

We've said before, and we're sure you agree, that your true wealth is measured by much more than just your net worth. How can your estate plan go beyond making sure your real estate, bank and investment accounts, and the rest of your financial wealth make it into the hands of your children, grandchildren, and future generations?

Ensuring Personal Possessions Make Their Way Into the Right Hands

One way that the Legacy Wealth Planning process goes beyond the traditional, narrow focus on finances is that it includes methods for distributing your family heirlooms and treasured personal possessions. These are the items, like your grandmother's tea set, your mother's wedding album, or your family photos, that are of immense importance to your family, even though they might not fetch a high price at auction.

They're the precious possessions you want to ensure make their way into the right hands so that they're preserved for future generations. They speak volumes about you and those who have gone before you, and they can communicate powerful messages about family heritage to future generations you may never lay eyes on.

Sadly, these are also just the types of possessions that stand the most chance of creating a family feud after you're gone, damaging or even destroying the relationships of those you love most. This is why, as part of the Legacy Wealth Planning process, you're given the tools you need to specify, in a flexible manner, who gets which treasured family heirloom or valued personal possession. Your attorney will discuss your wishes and needs with you, and will provide the documents necessary to make sure that your intentions are clearly communicated to your loved ones.

Passing on Your Family History

The final piece of the family wealth puzzle includes your personal wisdom and your family's history, stories, and folklore. These are the things that give your family its unique identity and set it apart from every other family in the world. This is also the part of the legacy you'll leave your children and grandchildren that will bring meaning and context to their financial inheritances.

We all know the memories and messages we want to capture and leave behind for our loved ones, but the task of actually sitting down and putting it all together in one place can seem overwhelming. Many people go to their graves with this task unfinished, and as a result, precious knowledge, insight, and wisdom vanish forever.

The Legacy Wealth Planning process allows you to preserve this priceless part of your legacy. It affords you an opportunity to put down in writing your personal biography, and the biographies of your spouse, your parents, and other family members. It also lets you record all the family stories and legends you hold dear, as well as your hopes and dreams for your children, grandchildren, and future generations. It gives you a way to communicate the hard-earned life lessons you've gained throughout the years that you want your loved ones to remember after you're gone. By preserving this information in a coherent and well-ordered manner, you can build on the foundation you've provided your family during your lifetime, passing on your values and morals, as well as creating a sense of belonging and family purpose for those who follow you.

At the end of the planning process, all of your documents, financial and non-financial alike, are compiled into a Legacy Wealth Portfolio. This puts your entire estate plan in one place so that it can be easily located and updated by you, and so that your loved ones can access it quickly in the event that they need it.

Chapter 35
The Most Important Part of Your Plan

When all is done, the help of good counsel is that which setteth business straight.

—Francis Bacon

Although we've touched on it, we have not yet discussed in detail the most important element of your estate plan, particularly when it comes to Legacy Wealth Planning. Based on our experience from meeting with our clients, we believe that the most important ingredient in the estate planning process is the *"right"* estate planning attorney. More specifically, the most important element in your estate plan is the relationship between your estate planning attorney and your family, and the security you gain knowing that:

1. Your attorney is specifically trained to protect your family's true wealth and to help ensure it is passed on and protected in the manner that best serves you and your loved ones.

2. Your attorney will be there when you need him or her, in the face of the myriad changes and challenges you are likely to face over the course of your life.

Your Attorney's Knowledge and Expertise

Any attorney can throw together a Will or a Trust for you, but this does not mean that the documents you receive will offer all the protections you and your family need. Believe it or not, not all lawyers have the training or experience required to act as trusted estate planning advisors, especially when it comes to complex issues such as minimizing your taxes or protecting your loved ones from creditors.

Focus
This is why you'll want to find an attorney who focuses his or her practice on estate planning. Estate law is a complex and ever-changing area in and of itself, and lawyers who simply draft the occasional Will or devote only a portion of their time to practicing in this area just don't have the time to stay on the cutting edge of knowledge and expertise.

Knowledge and Experience
Beyond simply finding an attorney who focuses on estate planning, you'll want to find an attorney with depth and breadth of knowledge and experience in the area. You should look for someone who has seen enough estate plans through, from start to finish, to understand what strategies work and what strategies do not. It is also a good idea to look for an attorney who has trusted and experienced colleagues on whom he or she can rely in the face of new or unusual situations. An attorney with a strong network of experts will be better able to find solutions to a variety of issues than an attorney who works in isolation and relies only on his or her own knowledge, experience, and insight.

Education
An estate planning attorney's education is important, too. In most states, attorneys are required to pursue a minimum amount of continuing legal education each year. Typically, the requirement is between 12 and 15 hours annually, and those hours can be in any legal subject, not just estate law. It is to your benefit to find an attorney who goes above and beyond this basic requirement. The American Academy of Estate Planning Attorneys, for example, requires that its member attorneys receive at least 36 hours of continuing legal education each year and that each of these hours is focused on estate tax, probate, and elder law.

In fact, only attorneys who are members of the American Academy of Estate Planning Attorneys are trained to engage in Legacy Wealth Planning and establish Family Wealth Trusts. The Academy offers intensive ongoing education and support for its member attorneys, helping them to provide the best possible level of service to their clients.

Trust

Once you've established that a potential estate planning attorney has the knowledge and experience to act as a trusted advisor to you and your family, you'll want to make sure that he or she is someone with whom you can communicate freely and someone whom you can trust. Your goal in finding an estate planning attorney should not be to simply have some reliable documents drawn up and leave it at that; instead, your aim should be to develop a relationship with your attorney so that you'll be able to rely on him or her when life's inevitable difficulties and changes visit you and your family.

Your Relationship With Your Attorney

When your Family Wealth Trust is in place, with all the necessary documents drafted and signed, you'll likely breathe a sigh of relief knowing that you've taken the right steps to protect your family. However, it's important to remember that estate planning is a process and not a one-time event. Life brings with it the inevitability of change, and we have found that, in the estate planning arena, changes occur in three basic areas:

- Legal changes
- Personal changes
- Attorney changes

When a change occurs in any of these areas, the validity of your estate plan can be affected; therefore, change calls for a review of and possibly an update to your plan.

Legal Changes

Estate planning laws are made and affected by a variety of government bodies, both on the federal and the state level. The most notable legal changes in recent years have come to us courtesy of Congress. For example, in 2006, Congress completely changed the rules governing Retirement Plans with the 900-page Pension Protection Act. A few years later, the Tax Relief Act of 2010 spelled a major overhaul of the estate tax code, which was closely followed by the American Taxpayer Relief Act of 2012.

The state legislature has authority over its own tax structure, plus Wills and Probate, Durable Powers of Attorney, and health care and HIPAA documents. With so much government oversight, changes to the law have the potential to happen at an alarming rate, and these changes can require adjustments in your estate plan.

Personal Changes

The government is not the only entity with the power to make changes affecting your estate plan. Your own family will experience growth and change over the years. Children grow up and get married. Grandchildren are born or adopted. Unfortunately, kids get divorced. The child who was a hopeless ne'er-do-well at age 16 grows into a responsible family man by the time he's 30. You can inherit a windfall or lose your shirt in the stock market. Family landscapes are ever-shifting, and this list of possible changes can go on forever.

In response to these personal changes, clients usually request modifications to their estate plans in three areas:

1. Beneficiary or Fiduciary changes to redefine who receives your assets or who is in charge of your assets in the event of your death or disability

2. Distribution changes to alter the way your estate is distributed (For instance, after learning about Legacy Wealth Planning, many clients want to change their estate plans to ensure that none of their Beneficiaries inherit assets outright.)

3. Asset changes to update your estate plan to ensure that all of your assets are owned in the name of your Family Wealth Trust

Attorney Changes
Finally, there are attorney changes. This is where your attorney redesigns your plan to bring it up to date. Strategies that worked in the past may not work anymore, or new strategies may evolve that serve you better. As we have mentioned before, tax law developments frequently occur, and may require us to re-think your plan. Beyond government changes, financial institutions often adjust their internal rules concerning what is acceptable in a Trust for accounts held by them.

If you have an ongoing relationship with your estate planning attorney, not only will he or she be able to respond effectively to changes in your life that impact your estate plan, but they will also be able to keep you abreast of changes in state and federal law as well as other policy shifts requiring an adjustment to your plan. This ongoing relationship will allow you to take full advantage of your attorney's knowledge and expertise and ensure that your estate plan uses the latest legal strategies to protect you and your family.

Conclusion

Do you remember earlier in this book when we discussed the defining moments of our lives? We identified our marriage, the births of our children, and the births of our grandchildren as some of those defining moments. We also mentioned that the deaths of our loved ones, especially our parents, were important moments in our lives. Defining moments often act as a dividing line after which nothing in your life is ever quite the same.

As hesitant as many of us are to think of such things, your death will serve as a defining moment in the lives of your loved ones. How will your family remember you? In too many families, death leaves a trail of disputes, court hassles, attorney's fees, and unnecessary taxes. As estate planning attorneys, we are the ones who see first-hand the anger and disappointment of surviving family members when they realize that Mom and Dad left behind loose ends rather than a coherent, effective plan. Sometimes the entire memory of a loved one is one of disappointment at the mess they left the family to clean up after their death.

The good news is that you don't have to leave behind a mess for your family. Each of us has the opportunity to arrange everything just the way we want it. You can be remembered as a good steward over all your assets—financial and non-financial alike—and as one who created a plan that worked. There need be no family fights, Probate, taxes, or wasted money when it comes to handling your estate.

In many respects, one of your defining moments is how you handle your planning before you're gone. This book can be your starting point. It contains much of the information you need to do it right. The big question is whether you'll take the necessary action to make sure your future, and the future of your family, is looked after properly.

We hope that you will choose to leave behind a legacy of security, certainty, and peace.

Frequently Asked Questions

Q: *Can I act as my own Trustee?*
A: Yes. As long as you are competent to manage your own financial affairs, you can act as Trustee of your Family Wealth Trust. If you are married, you and your spouse can act as Co-Trustees. In fact, most Family Wealth Trusts are arranged so that those who establish them serve as the initial Trustees.

Q: *What can I do with my assets once they're in the Trust?*
A: If you are the Trustee, you can do whatever you like with the Trust assets. When you establish your Family Wealth Trust, you will transfer ownership of your assets from yourself as an individual to yourself in your capacity as Trustee. This means that you will manage the Trust assets in the interests of yourself as Beneficiary. As a practical matter, you will have complete control over all the assets in the Trust and will be able to buy, sell, rent, or invest the assets as you see fit. As the person who established the Trust, you will also have the authority to change the terms of the Trust itself, or even revoke the Trust if you wish to do so.

Q: *Will I have to use an attorney every time I buy new assets?*
A: No. Once the Trust is established, you will take title to new property in your capacity as Trustee. This means that new property will belong to your Trust from the outset.

Q: *Can I transfer real estate into my Family Wealth Trust?*
A: Yes. Not only can you transfer real estate into your Family Wealth Trust, it is important that you do transfer your real estate into your Family Wealth Trust. This is doubly true if you own real estate in another state. Real estate left out of your Family Wealth Trust will likely need to go through Probate before it can be distributed to your Beneficiaries,

and when you own real estate in another state, this can mean multiple probate proceedings.

Q: If I transfer real estate into my Family Wealth Trust, will my property taxes increase?

A: No. You will not see a change in your property tax bill when you transfer real estate into your Family Wealth Trust.

Q: Can I name out-of-state Trustees or Beneficiaries?

A: Yes. The Family Wealth Trust is not subject to the same types of restrictions that some states place on Wills. This means that you can structure your Family Wealth Trust in the manner that best suits you and your loved ones, which includes naming out-of-state Trustees or Beneficiaries, if this is what works for you and your family.

Q: Where do I need to register my Family Wealth Trust?

A: Your Family Wealth Trust is a private document and, as such, it does not need to be registered anywhere, even after your death. However, if you transfer ownership of any real estate to your Family Wealth Trust, new deeds reflecting this transfer will be recorded.

Q: Are there any limitations on changing the terms of my Family Wealth Trust?

A: As long as you are alive and mentally competent, you can make changes to the terms of your Family Wealth Trust or even revoke it without penalty at any time.

Q: Can I create my own Family Wealth Trust?

A: No. A Family Wealth Trust is a complex legal document, requiring knowledge of estate law as well as federal and state tax law. Only a qualified and experienced attorney can create an effective Family Wealth Trust.

Q: If I move to another state, will I need a new Family Wealth Trust?

A: No. Your Family Wealth Trust is valid in all 50 states, as well as the District of Columbia. However, since a move to a new state represents a major life change, we recommend that you use this milestone in your life to have a qualified, experienced attorney in your new state review your Family Wealth Trust.

Q: Is a Family Wealth Trust only for married couples?

A: No. A Family Wealth Trust offers protection for you whether you're married, widowed, divorced, or unmarried. Regardless of your marital status, it allows you to avoid Living Probate and Death Probate, as well as minimize estate taxes. It also helps to ensure that your assets are distributed to the family members, friends, or charities of your choosing, in the manner you choose, and in a way that protects your loved ones' inheritances from creditors and divorce.

Q: Can any attorney create a Family Wealth Trust?

A: No. A Family Wealth Trust should only be created by an attorney trained in tax and estate law. It is important that you seek out an attorney with significant experience and expertise in this complex field. Any attorney you choose to create a Family Wealth Trust should not only be able to describe his or her background, education, and experience, but also give you detailed information on how he or she stays apprised of the frequent developments and changes in the law. We recommend that you choose an attorney who is a member of the American Academy of Estate Planning Attorneys. After all, your Trust will be the document on which you rely to manage and distribute all of your hard-earned wealth. You'll want to make sure the law firm you choose is both qualified and experienced.

Q: *Is a Family Wealth Trust only for the rich?*

A: You do not have to be rich to benefit from a Family Wealth Trust. In addition to saving your family the expense and stress related to Probate when you pass away, a Family Wealth Trust spares your loved ones the expense and emotional nightmare of Living Probate in the event of your mental incapacity.

Q: *What are the major disadvantages of a Family Wealth Trust?*

A: A Family Wealth Trust does not carry any major disadvantages. It allows you maximum control over the manner in which your assets are controlled and distributed in the event of your disability or death, and it affords you complete control over your assets while you are alive and mentally competent.

Terms

Administrator
A court-appointed representative responsible for managing the estate of a person who passes away without a Will

Beneficiary
An individual or organization designated to receive assets left in a Will, a Trust, an insurance policy, a retirement plan, or a payable on death account

Community Property
A form of property ownership between spouses recognized in certain states

In general, Community Property is property acquired by either spouse during the marriage. Spouses are considered equal joint owners of community property; however, this form of property ownership does not carry with it a right of survivorship.

Conservator
A court-appointed representative responsible for managing the financial affairs of a person deemed incompetent to manage his or her own finances

Estate Tax Exclusion
An amount of money or other property an individual is allowed to pass on at death without triggering the estate tax

Executor
A representative appointed to manage the estate of a person who passes away with a valid Will

Guardian

A court-appointed representative responsible for managing the personal affairs of an individual who has been deemed incompetent to manage his or her own affairs

Heir at Law (Heir)

An individual who is entitled to inherit from a deceased person on the basis of state law

HIPAA

Acronym for the Health Insurance Portability and Accountability Act, a federal law designed to protect the privacy of patients' medical records and health information

Joint Tenancy

A form of property ownership among two or more individuals which affords survivorship rights to the remaining owner(s) when a co-owner passes away; also known as Joint Tenancy with Rights of Survivorship

Will

Also known as a Last Will and Testament

A Will is a legal document in which an individual designates who will be responsible for managing their estate after death, what powers that person will have, who will inherit the Will maker's property, and how that property will be transferred to those individuals. A Will also allows its maker to nominate a guardian to care for minor children in the event of the Will maker's death.

Living Probate

The process through which a court appoints a guardian and/or conservator for a person who becomes mentally incapacitated and does not have an effective incapacity plan

Living Trust
A legal entity created during the lifetime of a Trustor (the person creating the Trust) to hold the Trustor's property, allowing Probate avoidance, incapacity planning, and the distribution of Trust property to chosen Beneficiaries at the time and in the manner desired by the Trustor

Personal Representative
A blanket term used by many probate courts to refer to either an Executor or an Administrator of an estate

Probate
The court-administered process through which a deceased person's Will is proven to be valid and through which property is transferred to the Beneficiaries named in the Will. Probate is also the process through which the property of a person who dies without a Will or Trust is distributed to that person's Heirs at Law.

Qualified Retirement Plan
A retirement savings plan that meets certain requirements of the Internal Revenue Code and is therefore eligible for special tax treatment

Required Minimum Distribution
The minimum amount of money that must be withdrawn annually from a tax-advantaged retirement account beginning in the year after the account holder reaches age 70 ½; also, the minimum amount of money that must be withdrawn annually by a Beneficiary who has inherited a tax-advantaged retirement account.

Successor Trustee
A person who replaces an acting Trustee in the event of death or disability

Tenancy by the Entirety
A special form of Joint Tenancy available to married couples in certain states

This type of property ownership carries with it a right of survivorship and may confer additional protection from creditors.

Tenancy in Common
A form of property co-ownership that does not include a right of survivorship

Trustee
The person responsible for managing the assets held by a Trust for the benefit of the Trust Beneficiaries and according to the written instructions established by the Trustor

Trustor
The person who creates a Trust and transfers assets into it; also known as the Trust's *"Grantor"* or *"Settlor"*

Unlimited Marital Deduction
An IRS provision that allows an individual to transfer an unlimited amount of property to his or her spouse without paying gift or estate tax

Notes

? Medicaid Trust Plan

Notes

Notes

Notes

Buy *Legacy Wealth Planning for Minnesota and North Dakota Families* in Bulk

**Interested in purchasing
additional copies of this title?**

**Special discounted pricing
for bulk sales is available.**

**For more information,
please contact German Law Group at:**

info@germanlawgroup.com